W9-ATF-910

JEWS in AMERICA
A CARTOON HISTORY

Updated and Expanded

Montanis Family Library
D'Youville Cottage

JEWS in AMERICA
A CARTOON HISTORY

Updated and Expanded

DAVID GANTZ

THE JEWISH PUBLICATION SOCIETY
PHILADELPHIA, PA
2006 · 5766

Copyright © 2001 by David Gantz

First edition 2001. Revised edition 2006. All rights reserved.

No part of this book may be reproduced or transmitted in any form or by any means,
electronic or mechanical, including photocopy, recording, or any information storage
or retrieval system, except for brief passages in connection with critical review,
without written permission in writing from the publisher:

The Jewish Publication Society
2100 Arch Street, 2nd Floor
Philadelphia, PA 19103
www.jewishpub.org

Composition by Book Design Studio
Cover art by David Gantz
Printed in China

06 07 08 09 10 11   10 9 8 7 6 5 4 3 2 1

Library of Congress Cataloging-in-Publication Data

Gantz, David.
Jews in America: A Cartoon History / written and illustrated by David Gantz.
p. cm,

ISBN: 0-8276-0716-4 (original ed.)

ISBN: 0-8276-0828-4 (revised ed.)

1. Jews—United States—History—Comic book, strips, etc.
2. Jews—United States—Humor.
3. Caricatures and carttons—United States. I. Title.

E184.35.G36 2001
973'.04924'00222—dc21

2001029352

E184.35
.G36
2006

TO MY WIFE, DORIS, CHILDREN, ELLIOT AND ROBIN, MY GRANDCHILDREN, TARA, GABRIELLE, ERIN, AMANDA, AND SARAH, AND MY GREAT GRANDSON, ALASDAIR MACKENZIE GANTZ NEWMAN.

E184.35
.G36
2006

A WORD OF THANKS

The vision for this book came from Bruce Black, former children's book editor at The Jewish Publication Society. It was he who suggested that I create a comic book history of the Jews in America, but it was Ellen Frankel, editor-in chief and CEO, who recognized that my art and humor also would be appreciated by adult readers. Dr. Frankel and editorial committee chairman Chaim Potok worked closely with me in shaping the text and fine tuning the illustrations. Their guidance was essential and deeply appreciated. Carol Hupping, Sydelle Zove, and Robin Norman, on the Society's staff, also steered the development of this book, tending to the editorial and production details.

I also wish to thank the following individuals whose inspiration was critical: Clara Feldman, with her passionate interest in all things Jewish, and her daughter, Karen; Tara Gantz Newman for rapidly faxing me computer verification of many queries; and special thanks to my son, Elliot, to Shirley Gingold Sufrin, to Catsy and Sol Gantz, to Carol Erez, to Sol Krichevsky, and to Valerie Costantino.

JUN 1 - 2006

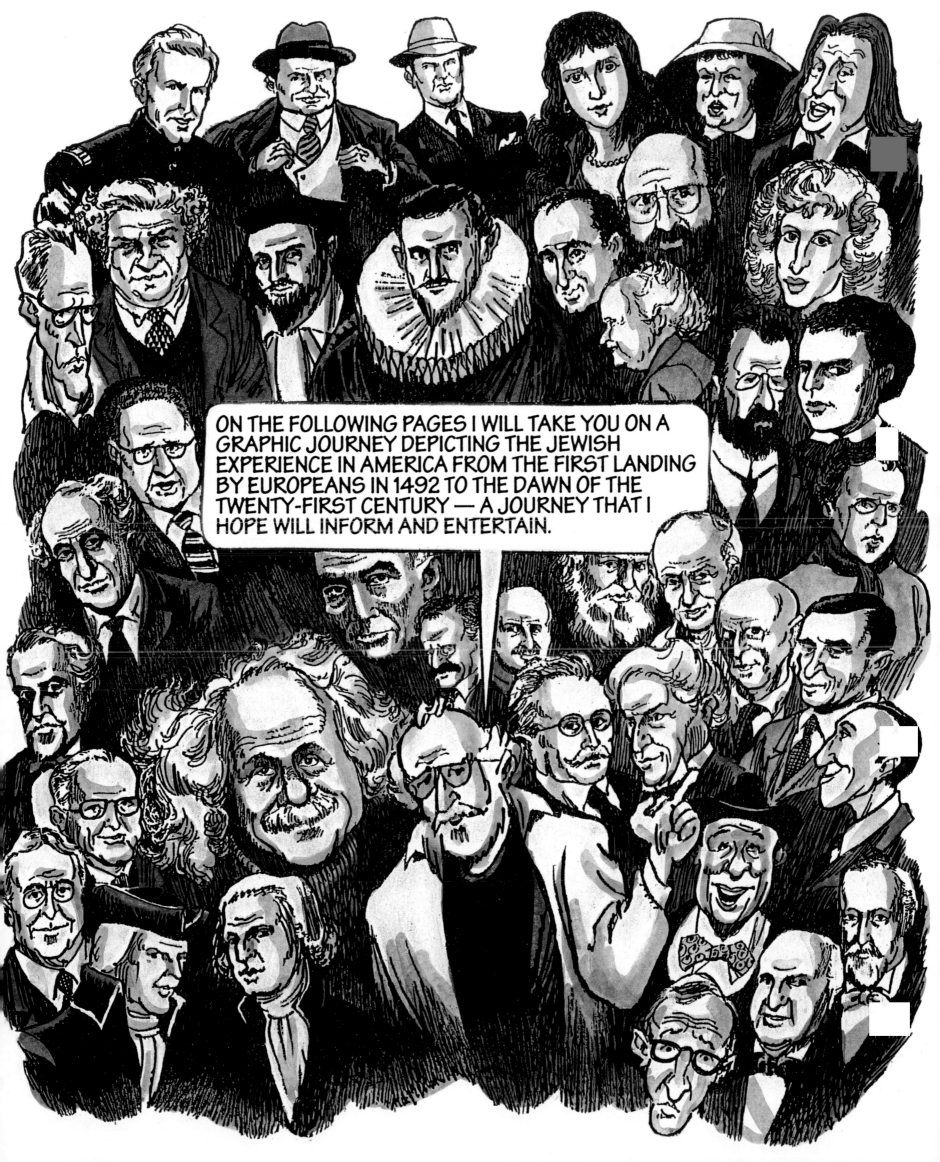

JEWISH LIFE IN EUROPE DURING THE TWELFTH AND THIRTEENTH CENTURIES REMAINED TENUOUS AT BEST, EXCEPT IN SOME PROVINCES IN SPAIN UNDER MOORISH RULE AND OTHERS UNDER THE RULE OF PEDRO OF CASTILE. JEWS ROSE TO HIGH POSITIONS IN COURT, COMMERCE, AND MEDICINE UNTIL THE REIGN OF FERDINAND AND ISABELLA.

1492

SPAIN'S JEWS WERE GIVEN A CHOICE: CONVERT TO CATHOLICISM OR LEAVE . . .

JEWS PUT FORTH THE ARGUMENT THAT THEIR ANCESTORS HAD BEEN IN SPAIN FIFTEEN CENTURIES BEFORE THE CHRISTIANS, TO NO AVAIL . . .

ACCEPT BAPTISM OR LEAVE!

THERE WERE JEWS IN HIGH POSITIONS IN COMMERCE AND THE COURT WHO CHOSE CONVERSION AND LATER ROSE TO CONSIDERABLE STATURE WITHIN THE HIERARCHY. HOWEVER . . .

250,000 JEWS WERE FORCED TO LEAVE A LAND WHERE THEIR ANCESTORS HAD LIVED FOR 1,500 YEARS. THEY WERE ALLOWED TO TAKE WITH THEM NOTHING BUT THE CLOTHES ON THEIR BACKS.

IN THIS SAME YEAR (1492), A SEA CAPTAIN FROM GENOA CAME TO SPAIN TO CONVINCE KING FERDINAND THAT THE WORLD WAS ROUND, AND THAT IF ONE WERE TO TRAVEL WEST ACROSS THE GREAT SEA ONE COULD REACH THE RICHES OF INDIA.

CHRISTOPHER COLUMBUS

1500

PEDRO ALVAREZ CABRAL'S PORTUGUESE EXPEDITION TO BRAZIL HAD A CONVERSO ON BOARD: THE INTERPRETER, GASPAR DA GAMA.

GASPAR, WHAT LANGUAGE DO THEY SPEAK WHERE WE ARE GOING?

HOW SHOULD I KNOW?

BUT YOU ARE THE INTERPRETER.

I'LL FIGURE IT OUT WHEN WE GET THERE.

GASPAR DA GAMA

FERNAD DA NORANHA

1502

FERNAD DE NORANHA, A CONVERSO, TRAVELED TO BRAZIL WITH A FLEET OF SHIPS TO ESTABLISH A COLONY. MANY OF THE CREWMEN AND PASSENGERS WERE ALSO CONVERSOS. DE NORANHA BECAME THE FIRST GOVERNOR OF BRAZIL. SEPHARDIM EMIGRATED FROM EUROPE IN GREAT NUMBERS, AND BRAZIL REMAINED IN SEPHARDIC HANDS FOR TWO DECADES ...

the INQUISITION is EXPORTED to AMERICA...

JEWS OWNED AND OPERATED MOST OF THE SUGAR REFINERIES. HOWEVER, FOR ALL THEIR FINANCIAL SUCCESS, THEY STILL FELL UNDER THE SURVEILLANCE OF THE INQUISITION.

1630 THE DUTCH SEIZED PORTUGUESE BRAZIL AND OFFERED FREEDOM AND EQUALITY TO THE CONVERSOS. THEY PRACTICED THEIR TRUE RELIGION—UNTIL...

JEWS WERE FORCED TO FLEE. SOME SAILED TO HOLLAND, SOME TO THE WEST INDIES, BUT ONE SHIP MADE IT TO THE DUTCH PORT OF NEW AMSTERDAM.

WHILE THE SPANISH AND PORTUGUESE WERE BUSY IN SOUTH AMERICA, THE DUTCH WERE SOWING SEEDS OF DEVELOPMENT IN NORTH AMERICA . . .

BACK IN **1626** PETER MINUIT PURCHASED MANHATTAN ISLAND FOR THE DUTCH WEST INDIA COMPANY.

STUPID WHITE MAN. ALL THIS WAMPUM FOR A MOSQUITO-INFESTED SWAMP!

STUPID INDIANS. TWENTY-FOUR DOLLARS' WORTH OF BAUBLES AND BEADS FOR ALL THIS TILLABLE LAND!

1654 A FOOTHOLD IN NORTH AMERICA— THE YEAR THAT THE JEWS WERE BEING EXPELLED FROM BRAZIL, THE DUTCH OUTPOST OF NEW AMSTERDAM WAS SETTLED WITH PETER STUYVESANT AS ITS GOVERNOR.

1689 THE BRITISH, FOLLOWING THE EXAMPLE OF THE NETHERLANDS, ALLOWED JEWS TO LIVE, TRADE, AND WORSHIP FREELY ON BRITISH SOIL.

1700 JEWS WERE IN CONTROL OF A MAJOR SHARE OF THE SHIPPING INDUSTRY BETWEEN ENGLAND AND THE WEST INDIES.

BY 1776, JAMAICA HAD RITUAL BATHS, KOSHER ABATTOIRS, JEWISH SCHOOLS, AND FIVE SYNAGOGUES.

1700 FREEDOM of THOUGHT and RELIGION

"IF GOVERNMENT CANNOT GRANT THIS, CITIZENS HAVE THE RIGHT TO FIND OTHER RULERS."—JOHN LOCKE, ENGLISH PHILOSOPHER (1632-1704)

THE BUSINESS OF GOVERNMENT IS TO PROTECT THE LIVES, LIBERTY, AND PROPERTY OF ITS CITIZENS.

HOWEVER, SLAVES ARE PROPERTY, AND THE LOWER CLASSES ARE TO REMAIN SERVILE.

ALTHOUGH SORELY LACKING BY TODAY'S STANDARDS, LOCKE'S PHILOSOPHY, ESPECIALLY FREEDOM OF RELIGION, WAS A BIG LEAP FOR THOSE TIMES.

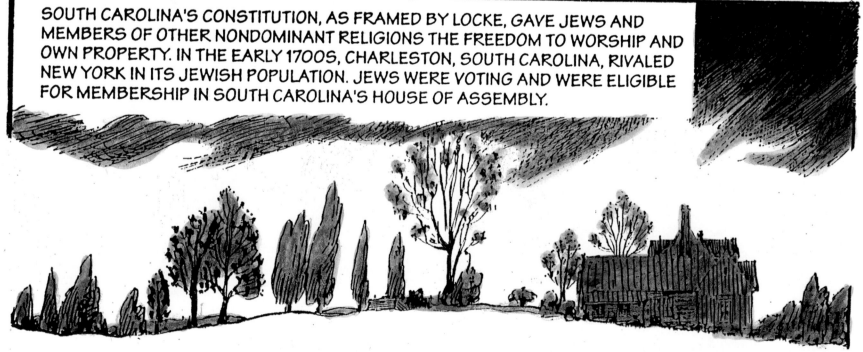

SOUTH CAROLINA'S CONSTITUTION, AS FRAMED BY LOCKE, GAVE JEWS AND MEMBERS OF OTHER NONDOMINANT RELIGIONS THE FREEDOM TO WORSHIP AND OWN PROPERTY. IN THE EARLY 1700S, CHARLESTON, SOUTH CAROLINA, RIVALED NEW YORK IN ITS JEWISH POPULATION. JEWS WERE VOTING AND WERE ELIGIBLE FOR MEMBERSHIP IN SOUTH CAROLINA'S HOUSE OF ASSEMBLY.

1740 The UNIFORM NATURALIZATION ACT

ALIENS QUALIFIED FOR CITIZENSHIP IF THEY WERE BORN IN AN ENGLISH COLONY OR HAD RESIDED IN ONE FOR SEVEN YEARS. THIS WAS THE FIRST JEWISH EMANCIPATION ACT ISSUED BY A MODERN EUROPEAN GOVERNMENT ESTABLISHING JEWISH SECURITY IN COLONIAL AMERICA.

I'M HERE EIGHT YEARS, ALPHONSE. HOW LONG ARE YOU HERE?

SEVEN AND A HALF; I'M A CITIZEN!

GREENHORN!

BY NOW, MOST JEWISH IMMIGRANTS WERE GERMAN OR POLISH (ASHKENAZIM). SEPHARDIM WERE DISTRAUGHT BY WHAT THEY BELIEVED TO BE THE UNCOUTH NATURE OF THESE STRANGE NEW ARRIVALS. SEPHARDIC JEWS CONSIDERED THEMSELVES IN A CLASS SUPERIOR TO THE ASHKENAZIM.

TO COUNTERBALANCE THEIR LOSS OF INFLUENCE BECAUSE THEIR NUMBER WAS DIMINISHING, THE SEPHARDIM TREATED THE ASHKENAZIM WITH SNOBBERY—UNTIL, HAVING GROWN TOO FEW, THEY INTERMARRIED.

PEDRO DE SILVA, MEET OUR NEW ARRIVAL, YOUR FELLOW JEW, YANKEL SILBERMAN.

VOOS MACHST DU, LANDSMAN?

YANKEL SILBERMAN?? THAT'S NOT A JEWISH NAME—AND HE DOESN'T EVEN LOOK OR SOUND JEWISH. WHAT KIND OF GIBBERISH IS HE SPEAKING? IT'S NOT LADINO

from THE PROMISED LAND to a LAND of PROMISE

1756 NOT ALL JEWISH IMMIGRANTS CAME FROM EUROPE...

*THE FOLLOWING STORY IS FICTIONAL. IT IS INCLUDED TO ILLUSTRATE THE FACT THAT ALTHOUGH THE MAJORITY OF JEWS SEEKING A NEW LIFE IN AMERICA CAME FROM EUROPE, SOME EMIGRATED FROM OTHER PARTS OF THE WORLD.

JUDAH ADWAR, A YEMENITE JEW WHOSE FOREBEARS WERE EXILED FROM JERUSALEM TWO THOUSAND YEARS AGO.

AS A CALLOW YOUTH OF SEVENTEEN, JUDAH ADWAR, BORN WITH AN INDOMITABLE AND ADVENTUROUS SPIRIT, SET OUT FROM YEMEN, THE LAND OF HIS BIRTH, TO TRAVEL BY FOOT TO JERUSALEM. JUDAH SUFFERED MANY A HARDSHIP ON HIS 1,500-MILE TREK THROUGH HOSTILE TERRITORY TO THE PROMISED LAND. THE SINGULAR WORD "PROMISED" SUGGESTED TO JUDAH THAT IN THE ANCIENT LAND OF HIS HEBREW FOREBEARS HE WOULD FIND A MORE COMPATIBLE ENVIRONMENT. BUT WHEN HE REACHED HIS DESTINATION, HE FOUND THAT PALESTINE UNDER ARAB RULE OFFERED LITTLE MORE THAN YEMEN. HOWEVER, THE ONE TREASURE THAT JERUSALEM ENDOWED HIM WITH WAS THE LOVE OF ESTHER HALEVI. ESTHER AND JUDAH SHARED A COMPELLING SPIRIT OF ADVENTURE.

AFTER THEY WERE MARRIED IN JERUSALEM, THE YOUNG COUPLE BOARDED A SHIP FOR AMERICA, THE LAND OF PROMISE, WITH THE DOWRY AND THE BLESSINGS OF THE HALEVI FAMILY.

THE SHIP MANAGED TO ELUDE THE BARBARY COAST PIRATES, BUT THEY WERE CAUGHT IN A FIERCE SQUALL OFF THE AZORES.

THE CROSSING OF THE ATLANTIC WAS MORE HARROWING THAN JUDAH'S TREK ACROSS THE ARABIAN DESERT. THEY ARRIVED IN THE PORT OF SAVANNAH IN APRIL OF 1778.

I WOULD HAVE CROSSED A DOZEN DESERTS IN PLACE OF THAT DAMNED OCEAN!

JUDAH, BE THANKFUL. WE ARE HERE IN THIS LAND OF PROMISE—OUR NEW JERUSALEM.

THE NEW ARRIVALS WERE WARMLY GREETED BY SAVANNAH'S SMALL SEPHARDIC COMMUNITY. JUDAH PURCHASED FIVE ACRES OF TILLABLE LAND WITH WHAT WAS LEFT OF THE DOWRY. THEIR NEIGHBORS HELPED THEM BUILD A LOG CABIN. JUDAH WAS IMPRESSED WITH THE SKILL AND SPEED AT WHICH THESE NEIGHBORS WORKED, AND THOUGH ESTHER WAS HEAVY WITH CHILD, SHE HELPED WITH CHORES. WHEN THE CABIN WAS FINISHED, THE ADWAR FAMILY SETTLED IN.

HASKALAH (ENLIGHTENMENT)

THE PHILOSOPHY THAT WAS TO SHAPE AMERICA AND BRING IT INTO CONFLICT WITH ITS COLONIAL RULER DIDN'T JUST BURST SUDDENLY UPON THE SCENE. EIGHTEENTH-CENTURY ENLIGHTENMENT HAD ITS ROOTS IN THE PHILOSOPHY OF MAIMONIDES AND SPINOZA.

MAIMONIDES
THE GREAT 12TH-CENTURY SEPHARDIC PHILOSOPHER

BIBLICAL MIRACLES CAN BE PROVEN WITH REASON BY WAY OF GREEK LOGIC.

DOES THIS MEAN THERE ARE NO MIRACLES??

OUR MERE EXISTENCE IS A MIRACLE!

BARUCH SPINOZA
17TH-CENTURY SEPHARDIC PHILOSOPHER

GOD AND NATURE ARE ONE.

GOD NATURE

GOD AND REASON EXIST SIDE BY SIDE.

MOSES MENDELSSOHN
18TH-CENTURY ASHKENAZIC PHILOSOPHER

GOD   REASON

NOWHERE ON EARTH WAS THE ENLIGHTENMENT MORE SUCCESSFUL THAN IN THE NEWLY FORMED UNITED STATES OF AMERICA. IN 1782, THOMAS JEFFERSON IN HIS "NOTES ON VIRGINIA" ARGUED THAT THE EXISTENCE OF A VARIETY OF SENSIBLE AND ETHICAL RELIGIONS WAS THE BEST GUARANTEE OF MATERIAL AND SPIRITUAL PROGRESS, AND OF HUMAN FREEDOM.

ON THE EVE OF THE REVOLUTION, JEWS IN COLONIAL AMERICA WERE THE FREEST JEWS ON EARTH!

GEORGE WASHINGTON (1732-1799)

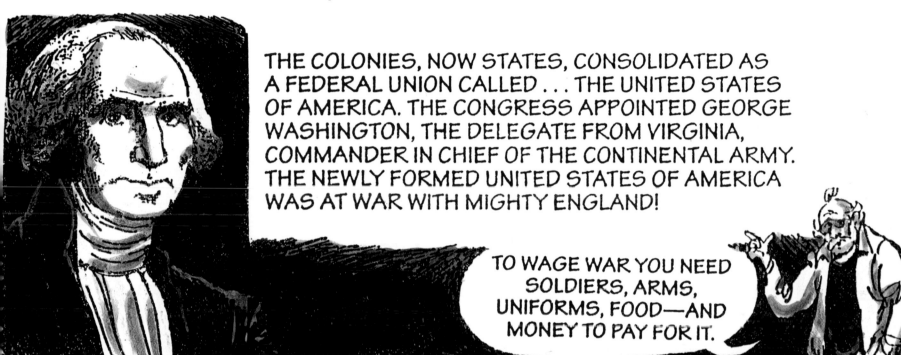

THE COLONIES, NOW STATES, CONSOLIDATED AS A FEDERAL UNION CALLED . . . THE UNITED STATES OF AMERICA. THE CONGRESS APPOINTED GEORGE WASHINGTON, THE DELEGATE FROM VIRGINIA, COMMANDER IN CHIEF OF THE CONTINENTAL ARMY. THE NEWLY FORMED UNITED STATES OF AMERICA WAS AT WAR WITH MIGHTY ENGLAND!

TO WAGE WAR YOU NEED SOLDIERS, ARMS, UNIFORMS, FOOD—AND MONEY TO PAY FOR IT.

GEORGE WASHINGTON MELTED DOWN HIS SILVERWARE FOR THE FIRST MINTED COINS.

HAYM SALOMON—POLISH JEW (1740-1785)
THE FINANCIER OF THE REVOLUTION

SALOMON HAD TO FLEE POLAND BECAUSE HE CHAMPIONED POLISH INDEPENDENCE FROM RUSSIA. AFTER IMMIGRATING TO AMERICA IN 1772, HE JOINED "THE SONS OF LIBERTY" AND WORKED TO RESIST BRITISH RULE. SALOMON, A BILL BROKER, NEGOTIATED CONTINENTAL BILLS FOR HARD DUTCH AND FRENCH CURRENCIES. SALOMON ASKED A MINUSCULE ONE-QUARTER OF 1 PERCENT FOR HIS SERVICES, WHICH HE NEVER RECEIVED. CONGRESS, IN APPRECIATION, APPOINTED HIM "BROKER TO THE OFFICE OF FINANCE." HAYM SALOMON DIED DESTITUTE AT THE AGE OF FORTY-FIVE IN 1785.

FRANCIS SALVADOR—THE JEWISH PAUL REVERE

SALVADOR, A SEPHARDIC JEW FROM ENGLAND, WAS ELECTED TO THE SOUTH CAROLINA HOUSE OF ASSEMBLY. ALTHOUGH BORN TO A PRIVILEGED CLASS, SALVADOR SIDED WITH THE COLONISTS IN THE REVOLUTION. IN 1776, WHEN THE BRITISH TOOK CHARLESTON HARBOR, THE CHEROKEE NATION, ALLIED WITH THE ENEMY, ATTACKED THE UNPREPARED COLONISTS. HOPING THE MILITIA WOULD COME TO THEIR RESCUE, THE SETTLERS WERE GIVEN REFUGE IN HIS MANSION WHILE SALVADOR RODE THIRTY MILES THROUGH HOSTILE CHEROKEE TERRITORY TO SUMMON THE AMERICAN TROOPS. IN THE ENSUING BATTLE, THE CHEROKEES AND THE BRITISH WERE DRIVEN OFF, BUT FRANCIS SALVADOR WAS MORTALLY WOUNDED. HE WAS ONE OF THE FIRST CASUALTIES OF THE REVOLUTIONARY WAR. ALMOST THE ENTIRE YOUNG ADULT MALE JEWISH POPULATION OF CHARLESTON SERVED IN CAPTAIN LUSHINGTON'S COMPANY. IT WAS KNOWN AS "THE JEW COMPANY."

MEANWHILE, UP NORTH THE BRITISH HAD GAINED THE UPPER HAND . . .

WASHINGTON AND HIS RAGTAG ARMY OF PATRIOTS SUFFERED A SERIES OF DEFEATS FROM NEW YORK TO PENNSYLVANIA. THE ENLISTMENT PERIOD OF MOST OF HIS MEN WAS ABOUT TO EXPIRE, AND HE NEEDED A VICTORY TO RALLY WHAT WAS LEFT OF HIS ARMY.

HESSIAN MERCENARIES, THE ELITE OF THE BRITISH FORCES, WERE BILLETED ACROSS THE DELAWARE RIVER IN TRENTON, WAITING FOR THE RIVER TO FREEZE OVER AND DELIVER THE DEATHBLOW TO THE REVOLUTION. EMPLOYING A DARING MANEUVER, WASHINGTON CROSSED THE RIVER ON A SUNDAY WHILE THE HESSIANS WERE SLEEPING OFF A DAY OF DRUNKEN REVELRY. HE CAUGHT THEM OFF GUARD, GIVING THE PATRIOTS A SORELY NEEDED VICTORY.

WITH AN ARMY MADE UP OF ONE-THIRD AMERICANS AND TWO-THIRDS FRENCHMEN, IT TOOK FIVE MORE YEARS FOR WASHINGTON TO DEFEAT THE BRITISH.

IN 1783, ENGLAND SIGNED A PEACE TREATY WITH ITS FORMER COLONIES, THE UNITED STATES OF AMERICA.

MAJOR NOAH'S ARARAT

BORN OF A SEPHARDIC MOTHER AND AN ASHKENAZIC FATHER, WHO FOUGHT IN THE REVOLUTIONARY WAR, THE FLAMBOYANT NOAH WAS APPOINTED A MAJOR IN THE PENNSYLVANIA MILITIA WHEN HE WAS EIGHTEEN. AT TWENTY-FIVE, HE PETITIONED PRESIDENT MADISON FOR A CONSULAR POSITION, SUGGESTING THAT HIS APPOINTMENT WOULD ENCOURAGE JEWS OF MEANS TO IMMIGRATE TO THE UNITED STATES. IN 1813, HE WAS MADE CONSUL TO TUNIS, WHERE SEVERAL AMERICANS WERE BEING HELD CAPTIVE.

MORDECAI MANUEL NOAH

HE CHARMED THE ARAB POTENTATE INTO RELEASING THE HOSTAGES. IN LINE FOR A COMMENDATION, HE INSTEAD WAS FIRED BY SECRETARY OF STATE JAMES MONROE, WHO CLAIMED THAT NOAH'S FAITH WAS A DETRIMENT IN A MOSLEM COUNTRY. HOWEVER, PRESIDENT MADISON, WHO WAS RUNNING FOR RE-ELECTION, SPENT CONSIDERABLE TIME IN WINNING BACK THE SUPPORT OF MAJOR NOAH AND HIS INFLUENTIAL JEWS IN THE DEMOCRATIC PARTY.

NOAH BECAME OBSESSED WITH THE IDEA OF ESTABLISHING A JEWISH HOMELAND IN AMERICA . . .

HE GAVE CONVINCING SPEECHES AND RAISED ENOUGH MONEY HERE AND ABROAD TO BUY A TRACT OF LAND ON GRAND ISLAND IN THE NIAGARA RIVER. HE NAMED IT ARARAT, "A COLONY FOR JEWS OF THE WORLD." ARARAT PROVED TO BE AN INACCESSIBLE WASTELAND. AMERICAN JEWS RIDICULED IT AS NOAH'S FOLLY. NONETHELESS, THE INDEFATIGABLE MAJOR NOAH MAINTAINED AN EMINENT POSITION WITHIN THE JEWISH AND GENTILE POLITICAL ESTABLISHMENT.

JEWISH MEN, ALONE AND COMPANIONLESS IN THE WILDERNESS, MARRIED CHRISTIAN WOMEN. WITH HARDLY AN EXCEPTION THEIR CHILDREN WERE LOST TO THEIR PEOPLE.

IN A LETTER TO HIS UNCLE IN ENGLAND, HAYM SALOMON, THE FINANCIER OF THE AMERICAN REVOLUTION DESCRIBED COLONIAL AMERICA AS A LAND OF "VEHNIG YIDDISHKEIT"—LITTLE JEWISHNESS.

THIS WAS SOON TO CHANGE WITH . . .

the POST-NAPOLEONIC UPHEAVAL and THE GERMAN-JEWISH INFLUX

IN 1789, THE BASTILLE WAS STORMED, IGNITING THE FRENCH REVOLUTION. THE OPPRESSED MASSES OVERTHREW THE ARISTOCRACY AND JEWS WERE GRANTED FREEDOM IN THE NEW FRENCH REPUBLIC. IN THE ENSUING YEARS THE ROYALISTS GAINED GROUND UNTIL NAPOLEON BONAPARTE SEIZED POWER ON NOVEMBER 9, 1799.

FOR A SHORT WHILE JEWS CELEBRATED THEIR NEWLY-FOUND FREEDOM . . .

HOWEVER, THE CELEBRATION WAS SHORT-LIVED . . .

NAPOLEON'S ARMIES MARCHED ACROSS ALL OF EUROPE ESTABLISHING THE PRECEPTS OF THE FRENCH REVOLUTION. HE TORE DOWN THE JEWISH GHETTOS IN THE COUNTRIES HE CONQUERED UNTIL HIS DEFEAT IN RUSSIA.

FOR THE JEW, A EUROPE DEVASTATED BY WAR OFFERED LITTLE MORE THAN A RETURN TO THE GHETTOS.

PEACE! FREEDOM! PROSPERITY!

AND ALL THAT GOOD STUFF FOR ALL!

EQUALITY

THE MASSES HAD TASTED EMANCIPATION AND THEY WERE NOT ABOUT TO GO BACK TO THE OLD WAYS. REVOLUTIONS BROKE OUT THROUGHOUT EUROPE. MANY IN THE VANGUARD WERE JEWS.

JOHANN GOETHE (1749-1832)

AMERICA, YOU HAVE IT BETTER THAN OUR OLD CONTINENT; YOU HAVE NO FALLEN CASTLES, NO STONES.
YOU ARE NOT INWARDLY TORN, AT A STIRRING TIME, BY USELESS MEMORIES AND VAIN QUARRELS.

THE GERMAN POET EXPRESSED THIS UTOPIAN VIEW OF AMERICA BEFORE THE CIVIL WAR. IT INSPIRED TWO MILLION GERMAN-SPEAKING PEOPLE TO IMMIGRATE TO AMERICA. MANY AMONG THEM WERE JEWS.

THE RUINATION OF THE NAPOLEONIC WARS PLUS THE ADJUSTMENT TO A PREINDUSTRIAL EUROPE GAVE IMPETUS TO THIS MASS MIGRATION FROM 1815 THROUGH THE 1820S.

1830 JEWISH IDENTITY in a CHRISTIAN COUNTRY
ISAAC LEESER—PRUSSIAN-WESTPHALIAN JEW

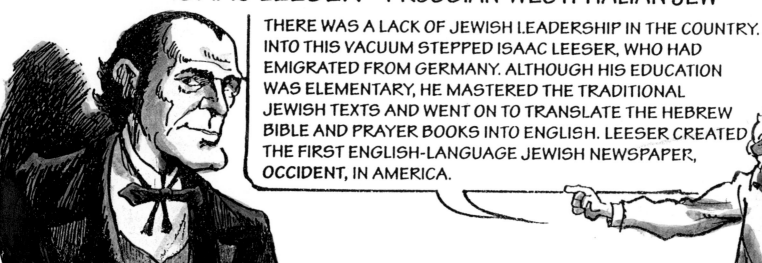

THERE WAS A LACK OF JEWISH LEADERSHIP IN THE COUNTRY. INTO THIS VACUUM STEPPED ISAAC LEESER, WHO HAD EMIGRATED FROM GERMANY. ALTHOUGH HIS EDUCATION WAS ELEMENTARY, HE MASTERED THE TRADITIONAL JEWISH TEXTS AND WENT ON TO TRANSLATE THE HEBREW BIBLE AND PRAYER BOOKS INTO ENGLISH. LEESER CREATED THE FIRST ENGLISH-LANGUAGE JEWISH NEWSPAPER, OCCIDENT, IN AMERICA.

PENINA MOISE—CHARLESTON-BORN SEPHARDIC JEW

OCCIDENT FEATURED POETRY AND MOST CONTRIBUTORS WERE WOMEN. MOST OUTSTANDING WAS PENINA MOISE. HER POEM "TO PERSECUTED FOREIGNERS" PRECEDED EMMA LAZARUS'S "NEW COLOSSUS" BY SEVENTY YEARS. THE LAST STANZA READ:

> RISE, THEN, ELASTIC FROM OPPRESSION'S TREAD,
> COME AND REPOSE IN PLENTH'S FLOWERY BED.
> OH! NOT AS STRANGERS SHALL WELCOME BE,
> COME TO THE HOMES AND BOSOMS OF THE FREE.

LEESER FOUNDED THE FIRST JEWISH PUBLICATION SOCIETY OF AMERICA.

THE PROBLEM of INTERMARRIAGE

REBECCA GRATZ—THE BELLE OF PHILADELPHIA SOCIETY

AT THE TURN OF THE CENTURY, THE GRATZ FAMILY WAS ONE OF THE MOST PROMINENT JEWISH FAMILIES IN AMERICA. THEIR PHILADELPHIA MANSION ATTRACTED THE ELITE OF THE SOCIAL AND LITERARY COMMUNITY AND WAS PRESIDED OVER BY THEIR BEAUTIFUL DAUGHTER, REBECCA. REBECCA FELL IN LOVE WITH SAMUEL EWING, A HIGH-BORN GENTILE WHO ARDENTLY PURSUED HER. ALTHOUGH OTHERS IN THE FAMILY MARRIED OUT OF THEIR FAITH, REBECCA REFUSED TO DO SO AND REMAINED UNMARRIED, DEVOTING HER LIFE TO PHILANTHROPIC CAUSES.

THE GREAT WRITER WASHINGTON IRVING BECAME ENTRANCED BY REBECCA'S CHARM AND BEAUTY . . .

WASHINGTON IRVING

SIR WALTER SCOTT

IRVING DESCRIBED REBECCA TO SIR WALTER SCOTT. ENCHANTED BY HIS DESCRIPTION, SIR WALTER MODELED HIS REBECCA IN IVANHOE AFTER HER. IN 1819, SCOTT WROTE TO IRVING: "DOES THE REBECCA I HAVE WRITTEN COMPARE WITH THE PATTERN GIVEN?"

ONE OF HER MOST NOTEWORTHY ACCOMPLISHMENTS WAS THE ESTABLISHMENT OF THE HEBREW SUNDAY SCHOOL SOCIETY OF PHILADELPHIA IN 1838.

FOR CENTURIES THE JEWS OF EUROPE WERE BARRED FROM ALMOST EVERY PROFESSION EXCEPT COMMERCE. JEWS WERE FORBIDDEN TO OWN LAND AND DENIED MEMBERSHIP IN CRAFT GUILDS. AS A RESULT THEY BECAME MERCHANTS AND FINANCIERS. THEY BROUGHT THESE VOCATIONS TO AMERICA. ALONG WITH THE EUROPEAN MIGRATION OF THE EARLY 1800S CAME THE BAGGAGE OF OLD PREJUDICES.

JEWS WERE SOMETIMES PORTRAYED AS TRICKSTERS, PURVEYORS OF FRAUD AND DECEIT . . .

. . . WHEN IN TRUTH MANY WERE HARD-WORKING MERCHANTS WHO CARRIED AS MUCH AS EIGHTY TO ONE HUNDRED POUNDS OF MERCHANDISE ON THEIR BACKS BEFORE GRADUATING TO HORSE AND WAGON. THEY BROUGHT THE AMENITIES TO THE NEWLY SETTLED FRONTIER.

THE FRONTIER JEWS

UNTIL NOW, IN CHRISTENDOM AND IN ISLAM, JEWISH FORTUNES WERE LIABLE TO SEIZURE AT ANY TIME. JEWS KEPT THEIR FORTUNES MIGRATORY AND THUS BECAME ADEPT AT TRANSFERRING CAPITAL. HOWEVER, WITH THE FREEDOM AND SECURITY AFFORDED BY THE UNITED STATES OF AMERICA THE JEW, PROTECTED BY THE EGALITARIAN NATURE OF DEMOCRACY, WAS FREE TO SEEK HIS FORTUNE AND BUILD ON IT ALONG WITH ALL OTHER CITIZENS. THE FRONTIER WAS OPENING UP AND OPPORTUNITIES WERE BOUNTIFUL. BECAUSE OF THE RESTRICTIONS PUT UPON THEM BY THE EUROPEAN GUILDS, JEWS DEVELOPED EXPERTISE IN ONE OF THE FEW VOCATIONS OPEN TO THEM—TRADING. THEY LOADED THEIR WARES ON THEIR BACKS, THEIR MULES, AND THEIR WAGONS AND HEADED WEST, SUFFERING ALL THE HARDSHIPS THAT THE NEW FRONTIER WOULD PUT BEFORE THEM.

POTS, PANS, TOYS, LADIES HATS, ELIXIRS, FRANKINCENSE, MYRRH, FLOTSAM AND JETSAM, AND SUNDRIES.

LEVI STRAUSS—BAVARIAN JEW

STRAUSS IMMIGRATED TO AMERICA IN 1848. AS A BACKPACKING PEDDLER IN NEW YORK, HE MADE ENOUGH MONEY TO BOOK PASSAGE TO SAN FRANCISCO, WHERE HE SET UP A DRY-GOODS BUSINESS.

IT FITS LIKE A GLOVE!

SHOULDN'T IT FIT LIKE AN APRON?'

HE THEN TOOK A FATEFUL TRIP TO THE NEVADA GOLD-MINING COUNTRY.

ANY LUCK DOWN THERE, PARDNER?

NOT YET, BUT I'LL KEEP ON TRYING TILL I WEAR OUT THESE PANTS— AND THEN SOME!

LEVI, REALIZING THAT MINERS NEEDED TROUSERS THAT COULD TAKE A LOT OF PUNISHMENT, WROTE TO HIS BROTHER IN NEW YORK . . .

Dear Brother,
There is a fortune to be made out here but not in gold. Buy up all the canvas and duck cloth you can get your hands on.

Zai Gezunt,
Levi

THE TROUSERS, WHICH HAD POCKETS REINFORCED WITH COPPER RIVETS, WERE A HUGE SUCCESS. STRAUSS WENT ON TO MAKE THEM IN DENIM AND "LEVIS" BECAME A PART OF THE AMERICAN LEXICON.

ARIZONA'S PIONEER MERCHANT FAMILY—

THE GOLDWATERS

MICHAEL GOLDWASSER

A POLISH JEW, GOLDWASSER WAS THE ELDEST OF TWENTY-ONE CHILDREN BORN TO A POSEN INNKEEPER. IN 1851, HE IMMIGRATED TO ENGLAND, WHERE HE MARRIED AN ENGLISH-JEWISH WOMAN AND ANGLICIZED HIS NAME TO GOLDWATER. IN 1853, HE SAILED TO CALIFORNIA WITH A YOUNGER BROTHER.

THE BROTHERS WORKED AS PEDDLERS AND MADE ENOUGH MONEY IN TWO YEARS TO BRING OVER MICHAEL'S WIFE AND TWO CHILDREN. THE FAMILY SETTLED IN SONORA, WHERE THEY OPERATED A GENERAL STORE/POOLROOM/SALOON ON THE LOWER FLOOR OF A BROTHEL.

↑ UPSTAIRS
ANNE LAZONGA
GOLDWATER
GENERAL STORE
← SALOON

GENERAL GRANT'S FAMILY WAS HEAVILY INVOLVED IN THE BLACK-MARKET COTTON TRADE IN TENNESSEE, MISSISSIPPI, AND KENTUCKY. JEWISH TRADERS, ALTHOUGH THEY CONSTITUTED A DISTINCT MINORITY, WERE SINGLED OUT AS THE MAJOR CULPRITS. GENERAL WILLIAM TECUMSEH SHERMAN COMPLAINED OF "SWARMS OF JEWS" IMPEDING HIS ADVANCE.

JULY 1862

DECEMBER 1862

GENERAL GRANT DECLARED, "THE JEWS VIOLATED EVERY REGULATION OF TRADE ESTABLISHED BY THE TREASURY DEPARTMENT." AND ORDERED THEM EXPELLED.

VETERAN SETTLERS OF THE TERRITORY—MEN, WOMEN, AND CHILDREN—WERE GIVEN TWENTY-FOUR HOURS TO LEAVE THE TERRITORY OF TENNESSEE, MISSISSIPPI, AND KENTUCKY. THEY LEFT BEHIND HOMES, BUSINESSES, AND CHATTEL IN A TREATMENT COMPARABLE TO THE INTERNMENT OF JAPANESE-AMERICANS IN 1942.

1863

THOUGH IT HAD RARELY BEFORE HAPPENED, JEWS REACTED COMMUNALLY TO A CHALLENGE TO THEIR CONSTITUTIONAL RIGHTS. IN 1863, PRESIDENT LINCOLN RESCINDED GENERAL GRANT'S ORDER.

The LUBAVITCHER and ULYSSES S. GRANT

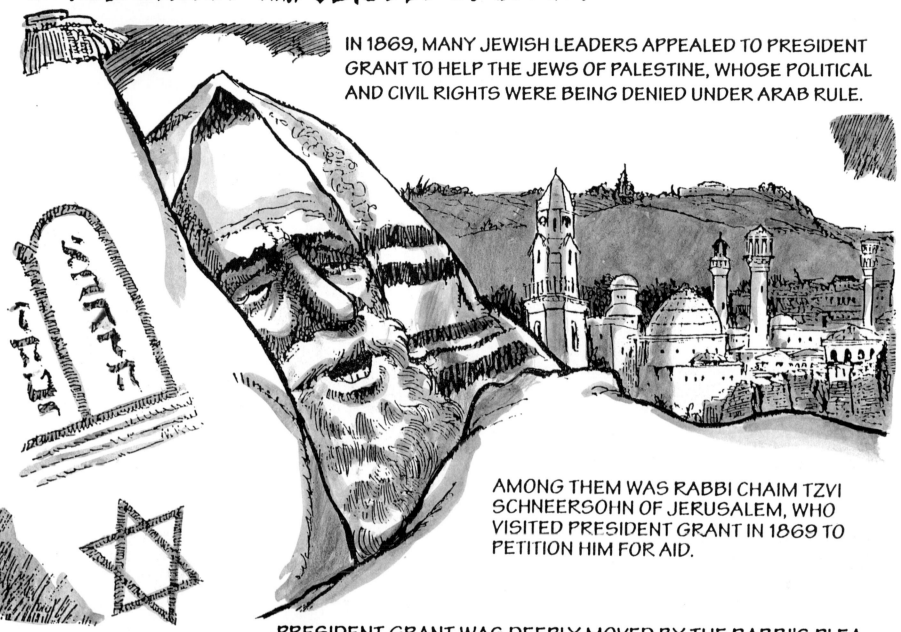

IN 1869, MANY JEWISH LEADERS APPEALED TO PRESIDENT GRANT TO HELP THE JEWS OF PALESTINE, WHOSE POLITICAL AND CIVIL RIGHTS WERE BEING DENIED UNDER ARAB RULE.

AMONG THEM WAS RABBI CHAIM TZVI SCHNEERSOHN OF JERUSALEM, WHO VISITED PRESIDENT GRANT IN 1869 TO PETITION HIM FOR AID.

PRESIDENT GRANT WAS DEEPLY MOVED BY THE RABBI'S PLEA . . .

I WILL LOOK INTO THIS MATTER WITH GREAT CARE.

POST CIVIL WAR ANTISEMITISM

RUMORS OF CIVIL WAR PROFITEERING LED TO POSTWAR ANTI-SEMITISM. THIS WAS AGGRAVATED BY A WAVE OF WRETCHEDLY POOR POLISH- AND RUSSIAN-JEWISH IMMIGRANTS. THE ASSIMILATED PREWAR GERMAN JEWS WERE APPALLED BY THESE NEW ARRIVALS. HOWEVER, THOUGH THEY KEPT THEMSELVES AT A DISTANCE, GERMAN JEWS SET UP PHILANTHROPIC AGENCIES TO AID THE NEWCOMERS.

EMMA LAZARUS (1849-1887)

EMMA LAZARUS'S WORK WAS IMBUED WITH A PASSION FOR THE ANCIENT HEBREW CULTURE PLUS A HUMANITARIAN EMPATHY FOR THE **PLIGHT** OF THE SURVIVORS OF THE BLOODY RUSSIAN POGROMS.

I HOPE WE ARE NOT PERCEIVED AS THEM!

HOW COULD WE? WE ARE NOT THOSE KIND OF JEWS!

LAZARUS SAW IN THESE HUDDLED MASSES THE BUILDING BLOCKS OF AMERICAN AND WORLD JEWRY.

EMMA LAZARUS WAS THE FIRST JEW TO ACHIEVE A LASTING EMINENCE IN AMERICAN LITERATURE.

THE REFORM MOVEMENT

EASTERN EUROPE GAVE BIRTH TO A RICH JEWISH CULTURE RANGING FROM RELIGIOUS TRADITIONALISM TO SECULARISM, PLUS A VARIETY OF REVOLUTIONARY SOCIAL THEORIES.

IN THE YEARS IMMEDIATELY FOLLOWING THE CIVIL WAR. REFORM JUDAISM, WHICH HAD ITS ROOTS IN GERMANY, BECAME DOMINANT. THE GERMAN-JEWISH ENLIGHTENMENT SET THE TONE FOR THE TIME.

THE REFORM MOVEMENT REJECTED THE RULES OF DIET AND PURITY IN DRESS, AND ASSERTED THAT JEWS WERE NO LONGER A NATION BUT A RELIGIOUS COMMUNITY.

IT WAS LIBERAL, RATIONAL, RESTRAINED, AND PATRIOTIC.

THE MOVEMENT INTERPRETED MESSIANISM AS A STRUGGLE FOR TRUTH, JUSTICE, AND RIGHTEOUSNESS THAT COULD FLOURISH ALONGSIDE OTHER RELIGIONS AND PEOPLE OF GOOD WILL.

ISAAC MAYER WISE (1819-1900)

ISAAC MAYER WISE IMMIGRATED TO THE UNITED STATES IN 1846 AND BECAME THE PIONEER OF REFORM JUDAISM IN AMERICA. WISE FOUNDED THE HEBREW UNION COLLEGE OF CINCINNATI FOR THE TRAINING OF REFORM RABBIS.

READY-TO-WEAR and The JEWISH IMMIGRANT

ELIAS HOWE

ELIAS HOWE INVENTED THE SEWING MACHINE IN 1846. ISAAC SINGER PERFECTED IT IN 1850. ALTHOUGH THESE TWO MEN WERE NOT JEWISH, THEY HAD A PROFOUND EFFECT ON THE BURGEONING NEW JEWISH IMMIGRANT SOCIETY.

ISAAC M. SINGER

THE SEWING MACHINE, WHICH HELPED SPEED THE MANUFACTURE OF UNIFORMS FOR THE UNION DURING THE CIVIL WAR, LED TO THE EXPANSION OF THE READY-TO-WEAR CLOTHING INDUSTRY FOR CIVILIANS.

THE WHOLESALE AND RETAIL CLOTHING MARKET WAS DOMINATED BY JEWS WHO MOVED EASILY INTO THE MANUFACTURE OF READY-TO-WEAR. BETWEEN 1860 AND 1890, THE MANUFACTURE OF READY-TO-WEAR CLOTHING BECAME THE MAINSTAY OF THE JEWISH IMMIGRANT SOCIETY, WHICH WAS BASED IN NEW YORK.

THE READY-TO-WEAR CLOTHING INDUSTRY HELPED TO DEMOCRATIZE THE NATION BY BLURRING THE VISUAL DIFFERENCES BETWEEN RICH AND POOR.

THE CIVIL WAR BROUGHT OUT THE ORGANIZATIONAL SKILLS OF AMERICAN JEWS. FROM 1880 ON, JEWS BECAME A POWER IN BANKING AND INDUSTRY. MANY ILLUSTRIOUS JEWISH NAMES FILLED THE ROSTER: *SCHIFF, GUGENHEIM, GOULD, OCHS, SELIGMAN, ADLER, FELS, SULZBERGER, GOLDWATER, LEVI STRAUS, ABRAHAM and STRAUS, SACHS, LERNER, SCHENK, GOLDMAN, WARNER, PULITZER, GOLDWYN, SOLOMON.*

JOSEPH SELIGMAN (1819-1880)

BAVARIAN JEW

AFTER PEDDLING IN PENNSYLVANIA, THE SELIGMAN BROTHERS SET UP A STORE IN WATERTOWN, NEW YORK, WHERE JOSEPH FORMED A FRIENDSHIP WITH LIEUTENANT ULYSSES S. GRANT. THE BROTHERS WENT ON TO CREATE A CLOTHING MONOPOLY IN SAN FRANCISCO AND EVENTUALLY ESTABLISHED THEMSELVES IN BANKING.

IN 1877, JOSEPH SELIGMAN WAS THE MOST PROMINENT JEW IN AMERICA, AND A RESPECTED GOVERNMENT ADVISOR. IN THAT SAME YEAR, SELIGMAN WAS REFUSED ADMISSION TO THE GRAND UNION HOTEL IN SARATOGA, NEW YORK, WHICH WAS OWNED BY A. T. STEWART. SELIGMAN HAD TURNED DOWN PRESIDENT GRANT'S OFFER TO MAKE HIM SECRETARY OF THE TREASURY AND HAD RECOMMENDED A. T. STEWART FOR THE JOB. STEWART WAS REJECTED BECAUSE OF HIS TIES TO BOSS TWEED.

STEWART COULD NOT GET OVER THE FACT THAT A JEW HAD BEEN GIVEN PREFERENCE OVER HIM.

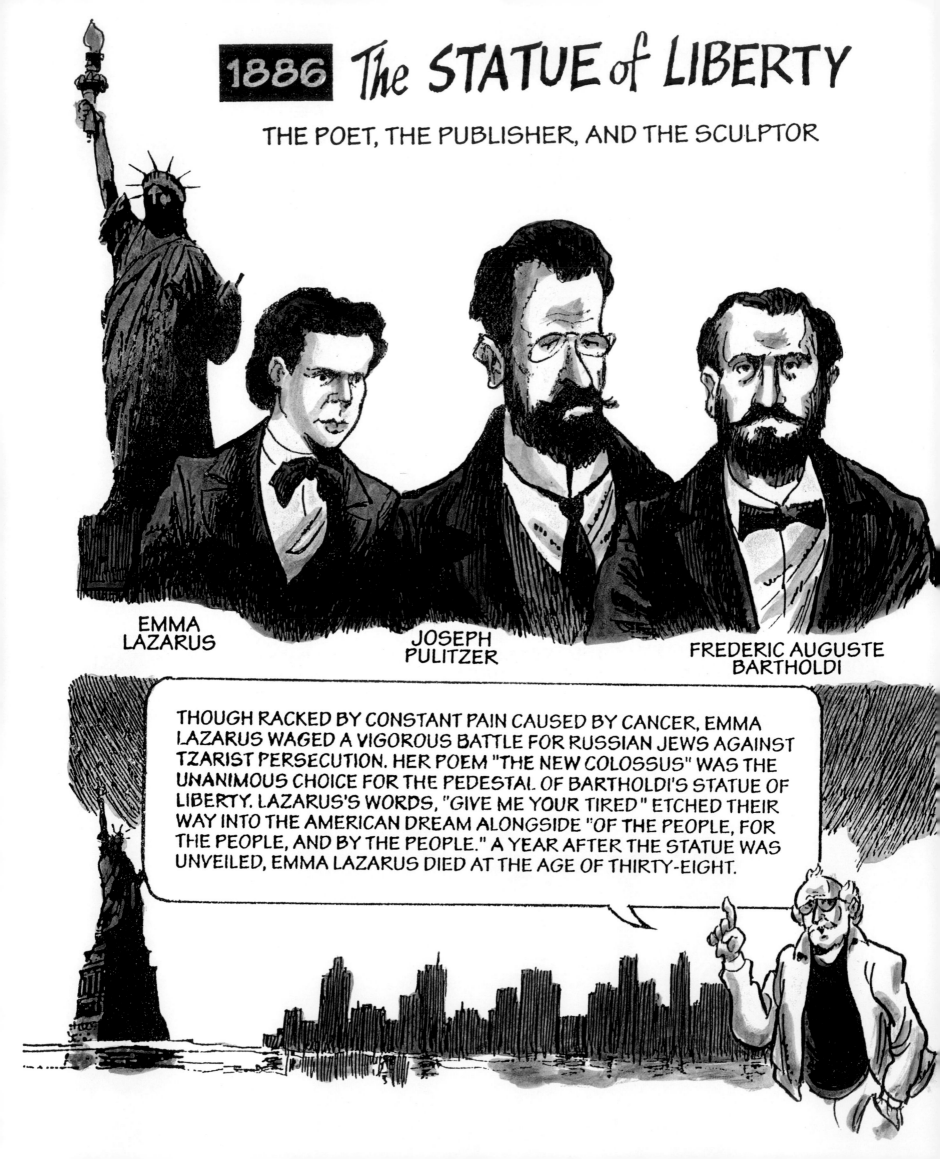

1886 The STATUE of LIBERTY

THE POET, THE PUBLISHER, AND THE SCULPTOR

EMMA
LAZARUS

JOSEPH
PULITZER

FREDERIC AUGUSTE
BARTHOLDI

THOUGH RACKED BY CONSTANT PAIN CAUSED BY CANCER, EMMA LAZARUS WAGED A VIGOROUS BATTLE FOR RUSSIAN JEWS AGAINST TZARIST PERSECUTION. HER POEM "THE NEW COLOSSUS" WAS THE UNANIMOUS CHOICE FOR THE PEDESTAL OF BARTHOLDI'S STATUE OF LIBERTY. LAZARUS'S WORDS, "GIVE ME YOUR TIRED" ETCHED THEIR WAY INTO THE AMERICAN DREAM ALONGSIDE "OF THE PEOPLE, FOR THE PEOPLE, AND BY THE PEOPLE." A YEAR AFTER THE STATUE WAS UNVEILED, EMMA LAZARUS DIED AT THE AGE OF THIRTY-EIGHT.

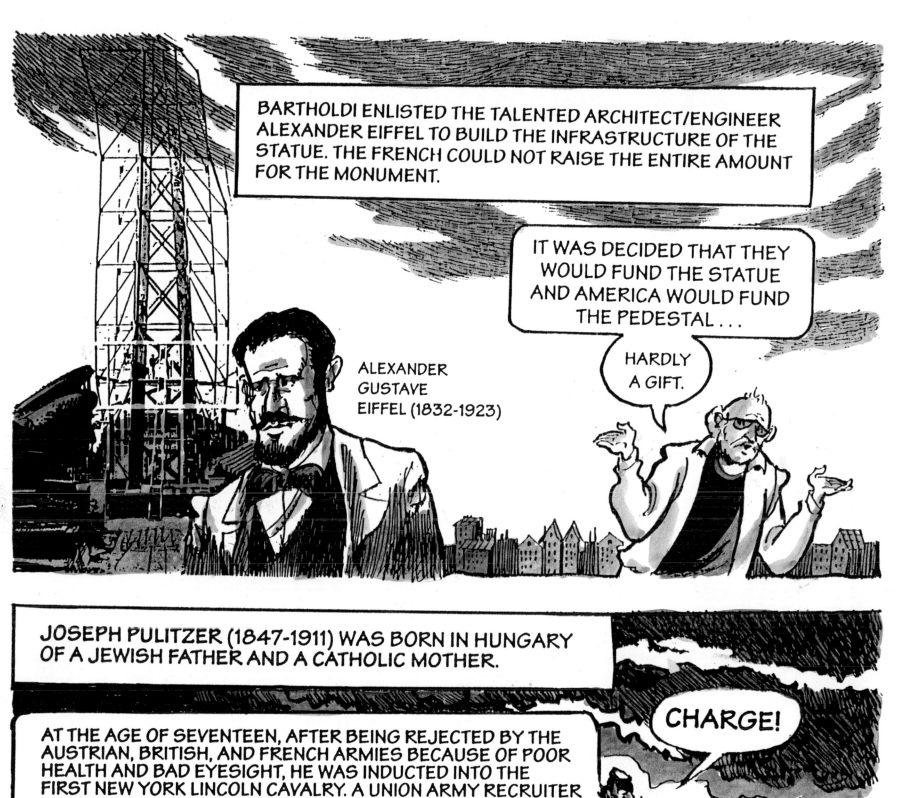

BARTHOLDI ENLISTED THE TALENTED ARCHITECT/ENGINEER ALEXANDER EIFFEL TO BUILD THE INFRASTRUCTURE OF THE STATUE. THE FRENCH COULD NOT RAISE THE ENTIRE AMOUNT FOR THE MONUMENT.

IT WAS DECIDED THAT THEY WOULD FUND THE STATUE AND AMERICA WOULD FUND THE PEDESTAL . . .

HARDLY A GIFT.

ALEXANDER GUSTAVE EIFFEL (1832-1923)

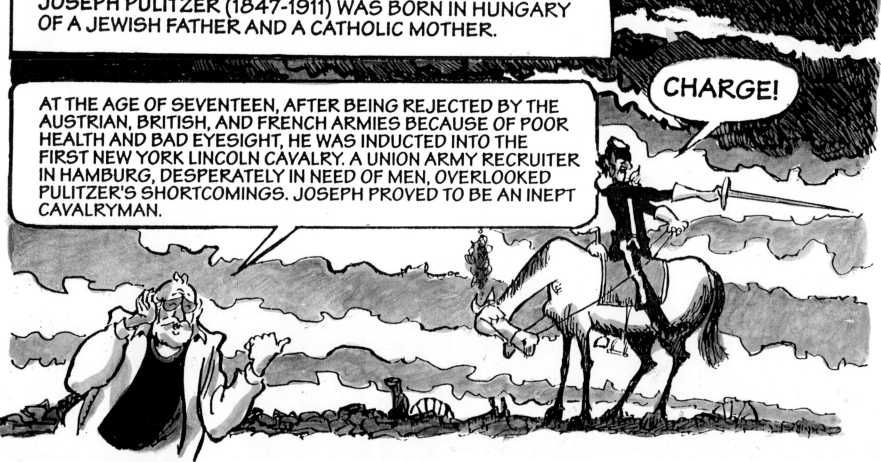

JOSEPH PULITZER (1847-1911) WAS BORN IN HUNGARY OF A JEWISH FATHER AND A CATHOLIC MOTHER.

AT THE AGE OF SEVENTEEN, AFTER BEING REJECTED BY THE AUSTRIAN, BRITISH, AND FRENCH ARMIES BECAUSE OF POOR HEALTH AND BAD EYESIGHT, HE WAS INDUCTED INTO THE FIRST NEW YORK LINCOLN CAVALRY. A UNION ARMY RECRUITER IN HAMBURG, DESPERATELY IN NEED OF MEN, OVERLOOKED PULITZER'S SHORTCOMINGS. JOSEPH PROVED TO BE AN INEPT CAVALRYMAN.

CHARGE!

AFTER THE WAR PULITZER BOUGHT THE FAILING PAPER, *THE WORLD*, WHICH WAS PUBLISHED IN NEW YORK. HE INSTITUTED THE FRONT-PAGE HEADLINE AND PLEDGED HIS PAPER TO OPPOSE THE PRIVILEGED CLASS AND SYMPATHIZE WITH THE MASSES.

MEANWHILE, THE STATUE REMAINED CRATED OWING TO LACK OF FUNDS FOR THE PEDESTAL. GOVERNOR CLEVELAND AND HOMEGROWN TYCOONS MORGAN, VANDERBILT, AND GOULD REFUSED TO CONTRIBUTE. PULITZER APPEALED TO HIS READERS FOR THEIR PENNIES. CONTRIBUTIONS POURED IN AND PULITZER LET IT BE KNOWN THAT SCHOOLCHILDREN'S PENNIES BUILT THE PEDESTAL.

1887

AS LUCK WOULD HAVE IT, THE DAY OF THE UNVEILING WAS GRAY, MURKY, AND FOG-SHROUDED . . .

MORGAN, VANDERBILT, GOULD, AND CLEVELAND ATTENDED THE CEREMONY ON BEDLOE'S ISLAND WHILE THE MASSES WATCHED FROM ACROSS THE HARBOR ON THE BATTERY. THE COMMON FOLK KNEW THROUGH EMMA LAZARUS'S "THE NEW COLOSSUS" THAT THE STATUE WAS DEDICATED TO THEM.

RUSSIAN POGROMS ESCALATE

NOTHING JEWISH IS ALIEN TO MY HEART.

JACOB SCHIFF—THE GREAT PHILANTHROPIST
GERMAN JEW (1847-1920) FINANCIER

AS A PROUD AND GRATEFUL AMERICAN, SCHIFF GAVE GENEROUSLY TO A MULTITUDE OF CIVIC ACTIVITIES AND PHILANTHROPIES. HE WAS A LARGE-SCALE CONTRIBUTOR TO THE RELIEF OF VICTIMS OF RUSSIAN POGROMS. THE TZAR'S HORRENDOUS TREATMENT OF JEWS LED SCHIFF TO BE PROMINENTLY ACTIVE IN THE CAMPAIGN TO ABROGATE THE RUSSO-AMERICAN TREATY OF 1832. HE EXTENDED A SPECTACULAR LOAN OF $200 MILLION TO JAPAN IN ITS WAR AGAINST RUSSIA (1904-1905).

THEODORE ROOSEVELT—THE GREAT REFORMER
(1858-1919) 26TH PRESIDENT OF THE UNITED STATES

CONTRARY TO INTERNATIONAL PROTOCOL OF NOT MEDDLING IN THE INTERNAL AFFAIRS OF SOVEREIGN COUNTRIES, ROOSEVELT, UNDER THE UNRELENTING PRESSURE OF JACOB SCHIFF AND HIS CO-RELIGIONISTS, INTERVENED WITH THE TZAR OF RUSSIA TO OPPOSE THE BRUTAL TREATMENT OF SHTETL JEWS.

The SHTETL JEW takes to NEW YORK

THE RUSSIAN AND POLISH JEWS COULD NOT ACCEPT THE WATERED-DOWN GENTILITY OF THE GERMAN REFORMISTS. THEY SHOUTED THEIR FAITH WITH EXUBERANCE AND HELPED TURN NEW YORK INTO THE GREATEST JEWISH METROPOLIS IN THE WORLD.

ALONG WITH THIS ORTHODOXY CAME AN UNLIKELY BEDFELLOW— SOCIALISM.

THE NEW YORK JEW BECAME THE ENGINE THAT WOULD EXERT ITS INFLUENCE ON WORLD JEWRY.

A CRISIS in IMMIGRANT ORTHODOXY

IN 1880, OF THE 200 SYNAGOGUES IN THE UNITED STATES, 190 WERE REFORM. TEN YEARS LATER, OF 433 SYNAGOGUES, MORE THAN 200 WERE ORTHODOX.

JACOB DAVID WILLOWSKI
(1845-1913)
LITHUANIAN TALMUDIST

BY 1900, THE LOWER EAST SIDE HAD HUNDREDS OF TINY HOLE-IN-THE-WALL "SHULS." THE NEW IMMIGRANTS WERE NOT ALL OLD WORLD ORTHODOX.

IN THE LATE NINETEENTH CENTURY, THE RUSSIAN-JEWISH WORLD WAS BUZZING WITH NEW POLITICAL AND CULTURAL MOVEMENTS: ZIONIST, LABOR-ZIONIST, SOCIALIST, AND EMIGRATIONIST.

THE RENOWNED "SLUTZKER RAV," JACOB DAVID WILLOWSKI, ON A VISIT TO THE UNITED STATES IN 1903, WAS APPALLED BY LOWER EAST SIDE SHOPS AND FACTORIES THAT WERE OPERATING ON SATURDAY. THE REBBE WARNED THAT PIETY COULD NOT SURVIVE IN AMERICA.

RAV WILLOWSKI MAINTAINED THAT JEWS SHOULD RETURN TO EUROPE, WHERE THEY COULD LIVE PROPER PIOUS LIVES.

CONSERVATIVE JUDAISM

SOLOMON SCHECHTER (1847-1915)

BORN IN RUMANIA OF HASIDIC PARENTS, SCHECHTER ROSE TO PROMINENCE AS A RABBINIC SCHOLAR. HE GAINED WORLDWIDE RECOGNITION FOR HIS RECOVERY OF THE CAIRO* GENIZAH. JEWISH HISTORY OF MEDITERRANEAN-AREA SOCIETY WAS REWRITTEN OWING TO SCHECTER'S SCHOLARSHIP.

*A REPOSITORY FOR OLD SACRED BOOKS AND DOCUMENTS.

SCRIPTURE SHOULD BE IN TOUCH WITH THE ASPIRATIONS AND RELIGIOUS NEEDS OF THE AGE.

SOLOMON SCHECHTER, THE FOUNDER OF CONSERVATIVE JUDAISM.

LOUIS MARSHALL

SCHECHTER COMBINED SCHOLARLINESS AND OBJECTIVITY WITH PIETY— BUT PIETY WITH FLEXIBILITY AND INNOVATION. IN 1913, HE FOUNDED THE UNITED SYNAGOGUE OF AMERICA, WHICH BECAME THE NATIONAL INSTITUTION OF CONSERVATIVE JUDAISM.

AGAINST THE OBJECTION OF JACOB SCHIFF AND LOUIS MARSHALL, SCHECHTER ATTENDED THE ELEVENTH CONGRESS OF ZIONISM AND THEREAFTER ENCOURAGED THE JEWISH THEOLOGICAL SEMINARY TO PURSUE ZIONIST ACTIVITY.

SCHECHTER MAINTAINED THAT INTERPRETATION OF SCRIPTURE SHOULD ADHERE TO CHANGING TIMES.

SOCIALISM

MY GREAT-GRANDFATHER WAS JEWISH.

SO'S MY ZAYDEH.

WHILE THE ACCULTURATED AND URBANE GERMAN JEWS WERE MAKING THEIR WAY UP THROUGH THE OPPORTUNITIES OPEN TO THEM IN AMERICA, JEWS IN EUROPE WERE BREAKING AWAY FROM THE CONSTRAINTS OF ORTHODOXY AND THE SHTETL ECONOMY. IN 1897, ONE HALF OF THE JEWISH POPULATION OF RUSSIA WAS LIVING IN THE BIG CITIES AND WORKING AS TEXTILE LABORERS, AND THEY WERE READING THE SOCIALIST WRITERS.

THE JEWISH SOCIALIST BUND ORGANIZED MORE STRIKES THAN ANY WORKING-CLASS ELEMENT THROUGHOUT EUROPE.

WE DEMAND WORKERS RIGHTS

STRIKE

UNION

BY THE PEOPLE AND FOR THE PEOPLE

WORKERS OF THE WORLD UNITE

THERE MUST BE A UNION

JEWS FROM THE PALE OF SETTLEMENT IN RUSSIA WERE IMMIGRATING TO AMERICA IN EVER INCREASING NUMBERS. WHILE MOST OF THESE NEWCOMERS CLUNG TO THEIR TRADITIONAL RELIGIOUS PAST, SCATTERED AMONG THEM WAS A NEW BREED OF YOUNG JEWISH RADICAL IMBUED WITH THE PHILOSOPHY OF MARX AND ENGELS.

TWO SOCIALISTS

THEY BOTH PARTED WITH SOCIALISM—BUT FOR DIFFERENT REASONS.

SAMUEL GOMPERS (1850-1924)
ENGLISH JEW

THERE IS NOTHING WRONG WITH THE FREE-MARKET SYSTEM AS LONG AS LABOR GETS ITS FAIR SHARE.

GOMPERS IMMIGRATED TO AMERICA IN 1863 AND WENT TO WORK AS A CIGAR MAKER. UPON WITNESSING THE DEPLORABLE CONDITION OF THE WORKER, HE STARTED A UNION, WHICH WAS TO BECOME THE MOST POWERFUL LABOR UNION IN AMERICA, THE AFL (THE AMERICAN FEDERATION OF LABOR).

GOMPERS BROKE WITH THE SOCIALISTS BECAUSE OF THEIR BELIEF THAT THE ECONOMIC SYSTEM HAD TO BE REORDERED TO ACHIEVE THEIR GOAL.

THE ONLY WAY FOR LABOR TO GET ITS FAIR SHARE IS TO DESTROY THE SYSTEM AND REORDER IT.

THE PRAGMATIST

EMMA GOLDMAN (1869-1940)
LITHUANIAN JEW

IN 1885, GOLDMAN IMMIGRATED TO AMERICA, WHERE SHE FELL UNDER THE INFLUENCE OF ANARCHIST PHILOSOPHY. HER LECTURES AND WRITING CONDEMNING CONSCRIPTION IN WORLD WAR I LED TO HER IMPRISONMENT AND DEPORTATION TO THE SOVIET UNION IN 1919, WHERE SHE FOUND BOLSHEVISM MORE REPRESSIVE THAN CAPITALISM. GOLDMAN CONTINUED TO ARGUE FOR THE FREEDOM OF THE INDIVIDUAL AND CHAMPIONED WOMEN'S RIGHTS, SEXUAL FREEDOM, AND BIRTH CONTROL.

DESPITE HER RADICAL ANARCHISTIC THEORIES, EMMA GOLDMAN REMAINS ONE OF THE SEMINAL FEMINISTS OF THE TWENTHIETH CENTURY.

THE IDEALIST

A-MEN TO THAT!

HOW ABOUT, A-WOMEN?

A CLASH of CULTURES

IN EASTERN EUROPE MOST LEGAL MATTERS WERE LEFT TO THE RABBI. IN AMERICA THESE DUTIES COULD NOT BE PERFORMED BY THE RABBI WITHOUT STATE SANCTION. CONSEQUENTLY A SPATE OF PHONY RABBIS APPEARED.

APATHETIC TO JEWISH AND AMERICAN LAW, THESE CHARLATANS PRESIDED OVER BOGUS MARRIAGES, GRANTED ILLICIT DIVORCES, AND DECIDED MATTERS OF INHERITANCE AND ADOPTION. ANYONE WHO COULD GET HIMSELF A SILK HAT AND A WHITE SHAWL, CARRY A CANE, AND DELIVER A QUASI-SERMON WAS CONSIDERED A RABBI.

IN 1889, THE ASSOCIATION OF AMERICAN ORTHODOX RABBIS BROUGHT OVER JACOB JOSEPH, THE HIGHLY RESPECTED CHIEF RABBI OF VILNA, TO BRING ORDER TO THE REIGNING CHAOS.

BUT AS IT TURNED OUT, RABBI JOSEPH'S MANDATE WAS CONFINED TO BRINGING ORDER TO THE LUCRATIVE KOSHER MEAT BUSINESS.

IN 1909, A SURVEY INDICATED THAT ONLY 23 PERCENT OF NEW YORK'S 170,000 SCHOOL-AGE JEWISH CHILDREN WERE RECEIVING SOME SORT OF JEWISH EDUCATION. EVEN TRADITIONAL JEWS PREFERRED TO SEND THEIR CHILDREN TO PUBLIC SCHOOLS WHERE THEY'D BE BETTER TRAINED FOR AMERICAN LIFE.

IN A TRADITION BEGUN IN EUROPE, RELIGIOUS TUTORING WAS ASSUMED BY THE MELAMMED, A RELIGIOUS TEACHER OF CHILDREN. THE MELAMMED WAS PAID A MERE PITTANCE FOR HIS SERVICES, WHICH WERE CONDUCTED IN YIDDISH, AND HE RELIED ON HIS STRAP FOR DISCIPLINE. RELIGIOUS TRAINING WAS TENUOUS AT BEST.

LANDSMANNSCHAFTEN ...

INFORMAL CLUBS OF IMMIGRANT JEWS WHO SHARED A COMMON TOWN OR VILLAGE.

A RATIONAL COMMON DENOMINATOR OF IDENTITY FOR JEWS IN THE NEW WORLD

THE NEWFOUND FREEDOM OF A DEMOCRACY DREW THE EASTERN EUROPEAN IMMIGRANT JEW AWAY FROM THE RELIGIOUS SHUL-CENTERED CULTURE OF THE SHTETL TO THE NEW SECULAR-CENTERED CULTURE OF THE "LANDSMANNSCHAFT."

ORIGINALLY FOUNDED FOR THE PURPOSE OF REMINISCENCE, THESE FRATERNAL ORDERS DEVELOPED INTO LABOR SUPPORT, BURIAL, AND INSURANCE BENEFITS ORGANIZATIONS. BEGINNING WITH THE LOCAL BIALYSTOK MUTUAL AID SOCIETY, THE LUBLINER BENEFICIAL CIGAR MAKERS, THE LEMBERG BAKERS RELIEF SOCIETY, ETC.—THESE LANDSMANNSCHAFTEN GREW INTO NATIONAL ORGANIZATIONS.

OF THE TWO MILLION JEWS IN AMERICA, MORE THAN ONE MILLION BELONGED TO SOME KIND OF LANDSMANNSCHAFT SOCIETY.

ARBITRATION!

A LIVING WAGE

8 HOUR DAY

THE LONGEST-LIVED AND MOST EFFECTIVE FRATERNAL ORDER WAS THE WORKMEN'S CIRCLE (ARBEITER RING), FOUNDED IN 1892 ALONG CONVENTIONAL SOCIALIST LINES.

THE WORKMENS CIRCLE

THE YIDDISH PRESS

EDUCATOR OF THE IMMIGRANT MASSES

BY 1910, ALMOST EVERY IMMIGRANT JEW IN A BIG CITY READ A YIDDISH-LANGUAGE NEWSPAPER PUBLISHED IN NEW YORK. THE NEW YORK FORVERTS (JEWISH DAILY FORWARD), UNDER THE EDITORSHIP OF ABRAHAM CAHAN, WAS SUCCESSFUL IN RAISING THE POLITICAL CONSCIOUSNESS OF THE IMMIGRANT JEW.

ABRAHAM CAHAN (1860-1951)
LITHUANIAN JEW

AFTER JOINING A SOCIALIST BUND IN LITHUANIA, CAHAN IMMIGRATED TO AMERICA. HE BECAME FLUENT ENOUGH IN ENGLISH TO WRITE FOR THE AMERICAN PRESS. CAHAN THEN MOVED ON TO THE YIDDISH-LANGUAGE FORVERTS. UNDER HIS EDITORSHIP THE PAPER GREW IN CIRCULATION FROM 6,000 IN 1901 TO 200,000 BY 1917, SURPASSING ALL OTHER YIDDISH PAPERS. THE FORVERTS RAN A POPULAR FEATURE, "BINTEL BRIEF" (COLLECTION OF LETTERS), WHICH WAS THE FORERUNNER OF "DEAR ABBY" AND ITS ILK.

*TROUBLES

THE JEWISH PRESS INTRODUCES CLASSIC LITERATURE TO THE MASSES

FORVERTS EDITOR, ABRAHAM CAHAN, WAS THE YIDDISH-IMMIGRANT WORLD'S ABLEST JOURNALIST AND GREATEST EDUCATOR. IN THE EYES OF THE IMMIGRANT, HIS WAS THE VOICE TO BE HEEDED. CAHAN NEVER FORGOT HIS RESPONSIBILITY TO THE JEWISH WORKING CLASS. HIS PAPER WAS WRITTEN IN CLEAR, CONCISE LANGUAGE, STRIPPED OF THE SNOBBISH, PSEUDO-GERMAN OF OTHER YIDDISH-LANGUAGE NEWSPAPERS.

THE JEWISH PRESS BROUGHT LITERATURE INTO THE IMPOVERISHED HOMES OF IMMIGRANTS BY TRANSLATING EUROPEAN CLASSICS INTO YIDDISH.

YOU GOT THE SAME TSORES WITH YOUR DAUGHTERS AS KING LEAR, EH, REBBE?

HOW DO YOU KNOW FROM SHAKESPEARE, BOYCHIK?

I READ THE YIDDISH TRANSLATION IN FORVERTS.

פֿאָרװערטס

AMERICAN JEWS READ THE WORKS OF THE GREAT LABOR POETS MORRIS WINCHEVSKY, MORRIS ROSENFELD, DAVID EDELSTADT, AND YOSEF BAVSHOVER IN THE YIDDISH PRESS.

THE POET LAUREATE OF THE LOWER EAST SIDE

MORRIS ROSENFELD
RUSSIAN-POLISH JEW
(1862-1923)

... AND HARK! THE LOUD SIGNAL HAS SOUNDED,
AND DEAD RISE AGAIN AND RENEWED IS THE FIGHT ...
THEY STRUGGLE, THESE CORPSES, FOR STRANGERS,
FOR STRANGERS!
THEY STRUGGLE, THEY FALL, AND THEY SINK INTO NIGHT.

IT WAS IN THE NEW YORK GHETTO SWEATSHOP THAT ROSENFELD FOUND HIS VOICE. HIS POEM "IN THE SHOP" WAS REMINISCENT OF MARKHAM'S "MAN WITH THE HOE" AND HAD A SIGNIFICANT IMPACT ON YIDDISH READERS.

WHEN ROSENFELD RECITED HIS POETRY THERE WASN'T A DRY EYE IN THE HOUSE.

BECAUSE OF ROSENFELD'S FREQUENT ILL HEALTH, HIS WIFE TURNED TO STREET PEDDLING TO SUPPLEMENT THEIR INCOME.

IN 1907, THE LABOR POETS WERE CHALLENGED BY A GROUP OF POST-BUNDISTS WHO, DISILLUSIONED BY THE FAILED 1905 REVOLUTION IN RUSSIA, DISAVOWED THE SOCIALIST MOVEMENT AND ADOPTED THE MOTTO, "ART FOR ART'S SAKE." AMONG THEM WERE THE POETS MOSHE LIEB HALPERN, ZISHA LANDAU, AND REUBEN ICELAND AND THE PROSE WRITERS JOSEPH OPATASHU AND DAVID IGNATOV.

FOR THE JEW, THE MOST LITERATE OF THE ETHNIC IMMIGRANTS, THE WRITERS OF THE GHETTO WHO WORKED ALONGSIDE THEM IN THE SWEATSHOPS AND LIVED IN THE SAME VERMIN-INFESTED TENEMENTS WERE THEIR SUPERSTARS, UNTIL . . .

The BIRTH of the YIDDISH THEATER

IN THE EARLY 1880S, THE PRINTED PAGE BEGAN TO EXPERIENCE A BRAND NEW COMPETITOR—THE FLESH AND BLOOD POPULARITY OF THE YIDDISH THEATER.

THEATER PRODUCTIONS WERE A BLEND OF CANTORIAL COMPOSITIONS AND KLEZMER FOLK MUSIC INTERMINGLED WITH PLOTS SPRINKLED WITH FRIVOLITY, BROAD COMEDY, AND SENTIMENTALITY. THIS RICH VARIETY OF MUSICALS, DRAMAS, AND COMEDIES PROVIDED A SORELY NEEDED DIVERSION FROM THE GRINDING DRUDGERY OF THE SWEATSHOPS, WHICH WERE THE CONSTANT THEME OF THE GHETTO POETS.

BY THE 1890S, THE YIDDISH THEATER HAD BEEN TAKEN OVER BY HACKS WHO WERE GRINDING OUT MUNDANE MELODRAMAS AND BANAL MUSICAL COMEDIES.

INTO THIS WASTELAND STEPPED TWO DYNAMIC PERSONALITIES . . .

JACOB ADLER
ACTOR/DIRECTOR

and

JACOB GORDIN
PLAYWRIGHT

ALL THEATER THAT IS CRUDE, UNCLEAN, AND IMMORAL WILL BE DRIVEN FROM THE YIDDISH STAGE AND REPLACED BY BEAUTIFUL MUSICAL COMEDIES AND DRAMAS GIVING TRUTHFUL AND SERIOUS PORTRAYALS OF LIFE.

ADLER COMMISSIONED GORDIN TO WRITE A PLAY FOR HIS NEW INDEPENDENT YIDDISH ARTISTS COMPANY. INSPIRED BY LES MISERABLES, GORDIN WROTE SIBERIA. THE JEWISH AND AMERICAN PRESS DUBBED GORDIN "THE YIDDISH IBSEN." THEIR SECOND PRODUCTION, JEWISH KING LEAR, ESTABLISHED THE YIDDISH THEATER AS A SERIOUS ART FORM. THEREAFTER, THE AMERICAN THEATER, FOLLOWING THE ADLER/GORDIN FORMAT, MOUNTED ITS OWN ENGLISH-LANGUAGE SHAKESPEAREAN PRODUCTIONS.

THEY BROUGHT THE BARD TO THE BOARDS OF THE YIDDISH STAGE.

AND THERE WAS COMEDY IN THE FORM OF MENASHE SKULNIK, "THE SENTIMENTAL CLOWN."

THE BEST LAUGH IS WHEN IT COMES WITH A TEAR.

WILLIAM SHAKESPEARE

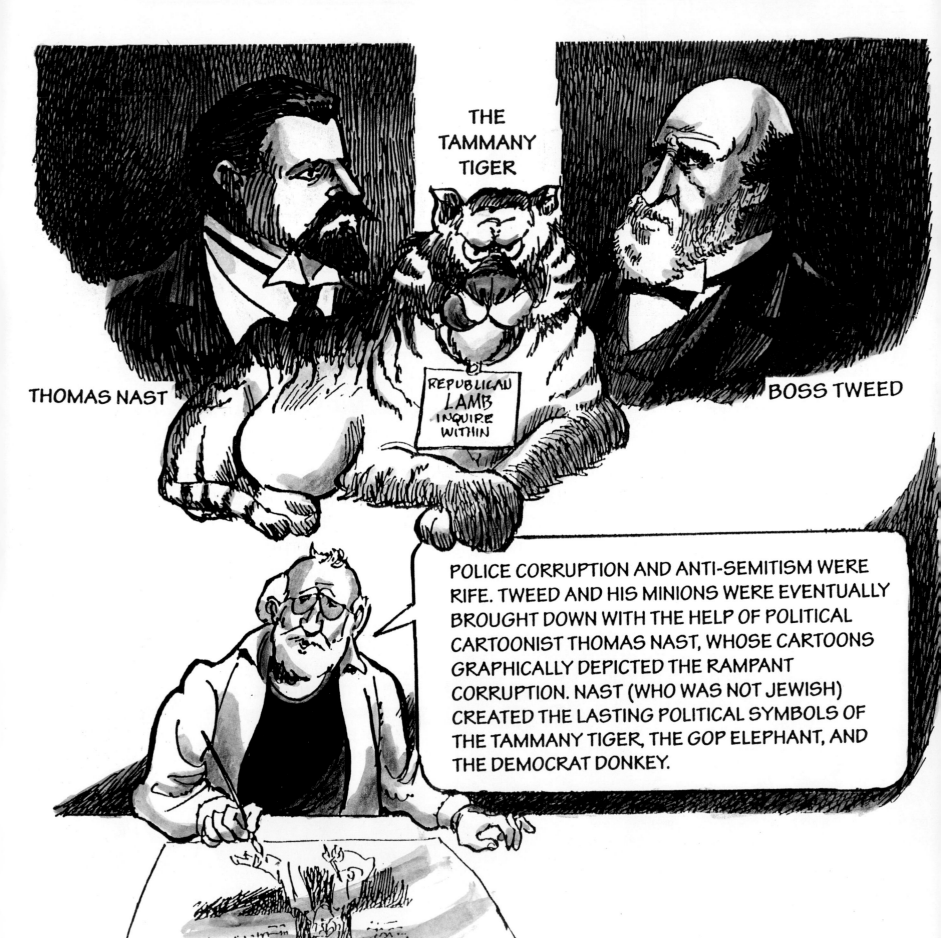

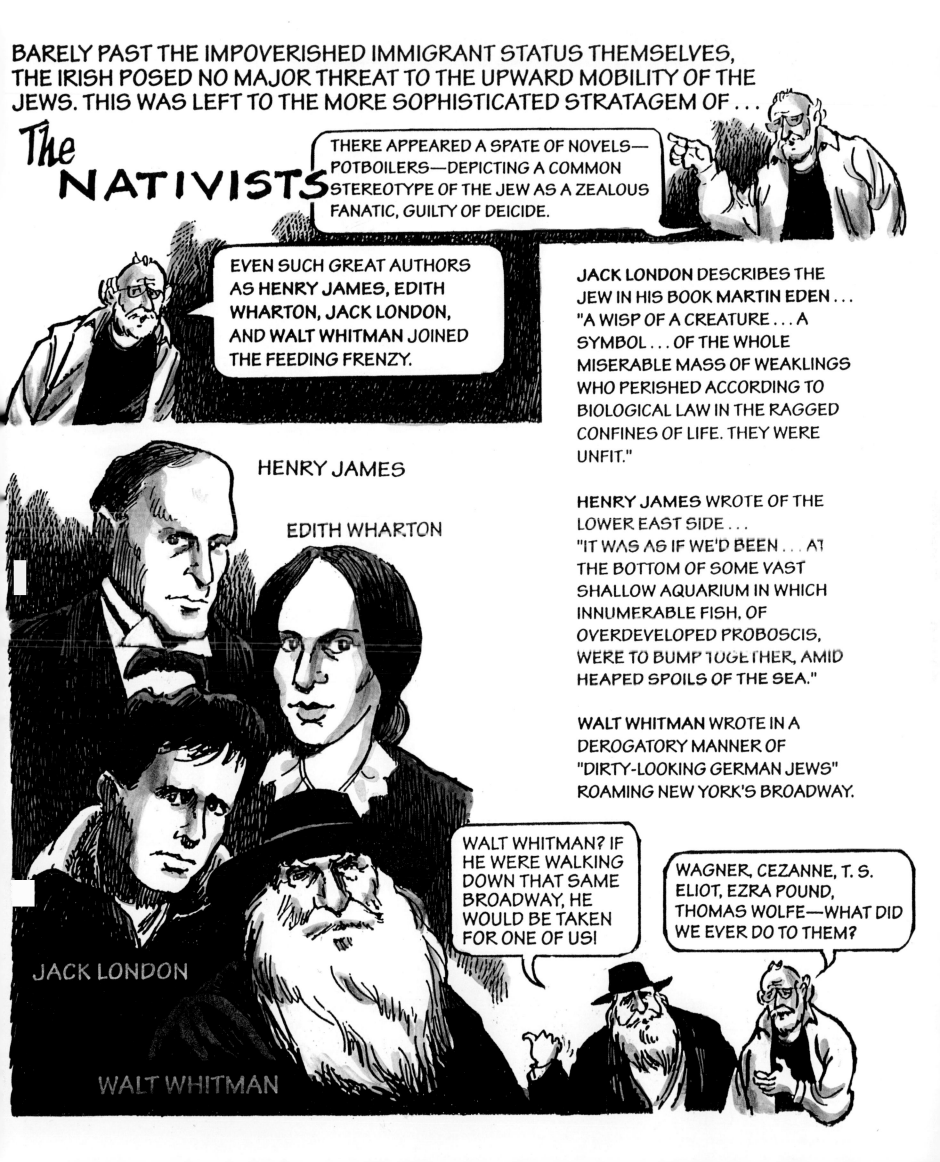

JUDEOPHOBIA

IN THE 1870S, JUSTICE WILLIAM STRONG OF THE UNITED STATES SUPREME COURT MADE AN EFFORT TO IMPOSE CHRISTIANITY ON THE CONSTITUTION. IN 1892, SUPREME COURT JUSTICE DAVID BREWER, WITH THE SUPPORT OF CLERGYMEN, A NUMBER OF GOVERNORS, AND ACADEMICIANS, ASSERTED THAT THE UNITED STATES WAS A CHRISTIAN NATION.

IN HIS SPEECHES, JUSTICE STRONG ASSERTED THAT JUDAISM WAS NOTHING MORE THAN A TOLERATED CULT.

AND ADD TO ALL OF THIS THE PANIC OF 1893.

AS THE ECONOMIC CRISIS OF THE 1890S DEVELOPED, THE HARD-HIT FARMERS AND SMALL-TOWN MERCHANTS COALESCED TO FORM THE POPULIST PARTY. THE POPULISTS BELIEVED THAT THE ROOT OF THEIR WOES WAS MONEY POWER. THEY CONCLUDED THAT THE SOURCE OF MONEY POWER WAS THE WORLD'S FINANCIAL CAPITAL, LONDON, AND THE HOUSE OF ROTHSCHILD.

YOU GREEDY JEWISH INTERNATIONAL FINANCIERS HAVE COST ME MY FARM!

FINANCIER, ME? FROM HIS MOUTH TO GOD'S EARS.

IT SAYS HERE: JEWISH FINANCIAL MANIPULATORS CONTROL THE WEALTH OF THE WORLD.

CAN YOU MANIPULATE US A HERRING AND A GLASS OF TEA?

THE WEALTHY ROTHSCHILDS WERE JEWISH. THUS, ALL JEWS WERE DEEMED PREDATORS AND THE IMAGE OF THE BANKER WAS FUSED WITH THAT OF SHYLOCK. AT THE POPULIST CONVENTION IN 1892, AN ASSOCIATED PRESS DISPATCH OBSERVED THAT THE MOST STRIKING THING ABOUT THE CONVENTION WAS THE EXTRAORDINARY HATRED FOR THE JEWISH RACE.

JEWS BATTLE RESTRICTIONISTS

JACOB SCHIFF KNEW THAT THE DISEMBARKATION OF IMMIGRANT JEWS IN NEW YORK AND OTHER LARGE EASTERN PORTS WAS THE CRUX OF THE PROBLEM. ONCE ASHORE IN THESE CITIES WITH SIZABLE JEWISH COMMUNITIES, NEWCOMERS EASILY BLENDED IN AND WERE DISINCLINED TO MOVE ELSEWHERE.

SCHIFF'S SOLUTION WAS TO TRANSPORT THE IMMIGRANTS FROM THE PORT OF DEPARTURE (BREMEN) DIRECTLY TO THE GULF PORT OF GALVESTON, TEXAS. THUS, NEWCOMERS WOULD HAVE TO SETTLE IN THE AMERICAN SOUTHWEST.

CASSEL

WHEN THE FIRST SHIP, CASSEL, ARRIVED, THE IMMIGRANTS WERE GIVEN A ROUSING WELCOME BY THE LOCAL RABBI OF GALVESTON, RABBI HENRY COHEN.

SCHIFF SET UP A FUND THROUGH THE JEWISH TERRITORIAL ORGANIZATION, AND MILLIONS OF RUSSIAN JEWS WERE TO BE MOVED INTO THE INTERIOR WITHIN A DECADE. THE ELDER STATESMAN OF THE JEWS WAS CONFIDENT THAT THE GALVESTON PLAN WOULD WORK BECAUSE HE HAD THE SUPPORT OF THE PRESIDENT AND THE SECRETARY OF COMMERCE AND LABOR, WHO HAD JURISDICTION OVER THE BUREAU OF IMMIGRATION AND NATURALIZATION.

IMMIGRATION INSPECTOR
A. HAMPTON

BUT THE 1907 FINANCIAL PANIC MADE IT DIFFICULT TO FIND EMPLOYMENT, AND IN THE SPRING OF 1910, THE PORT'S NEW FEDERAL IMMIGRATION INSPECTOR, ALFRED HAMPTON, A MILITANT RESTRICTIONIST, CHARGED THAT THE SCHIFF PROJECT WAS INSTITUTED TO EVADE THE EAST COAST'S MORE RIGOROUS INSPECTION PROCEDURES. TOGETHER THESE FORCES SPELLED AN END FOR THE GALVESTON PLAN.

EMERGENCE of a VICIOUS NEW STEREOTYPE

BY THE EVE OF WORLD WAR I, THE 3.5 MILLION AMERICAN JEWS HAD BECOME THE LARGEST JEWISH COMMUNITY IN THE WORLD AND THE RESTRICTIONISTS WERE BECOMING MORE FEARFUL OF THEIR GROWING NUMBERS. THEIR OLD STEREOTYPE OF THE JEW AS A FINANCIAL SHYLOCK BEGAN TO GIVE WAY TO A NEW STEREOTYPE.

IN 1903, A DIFFERENT BREED OF JEW (EVEN DIFFERENT FROM THEIR EASTERN EUROPEAN PREDECESSORS) WAS EMERGING. THEY WERE THE JEWS WHO HAD LEFT THE PALE TO SETTLE IN THE BIG CITIES OF EUROPE BEFORE EMIGRATING—AND THEY WERE IMBUED WITH THE CONCEPTS OF SOCIALIST EMANCIPATION. THEY INCLUDED SOME OF THE FUTURE LEADERS OF THE AMERICAN LABOR MOVEMENT.

THE OLD POPULIST STEREOTYPE OF THE JEW AS A FINANCIAL SHYLOCK GAVE WAY TO THE NEW STEREOTYPE OF THE IMMIGRANT JEW AS A BOMB-THROWING BOLSHEVIK.

The LYNCHING of LEO FRANK

THE RURAL SOUTHERNER'S PERCEPTION OF A JEW WAS THE POPULIST STEREOTYPICAL IMAGE OF AN URBAN, RADICAL, ALIEN INTERLOPER WHO WAS A THREAT TO HIS BIRTHRIGHT. NOWHERE IN THE COUNTRY WAS THERE MORE FEAR OF THE ALIEN THAN IN THE SOUTH. IN THE EARLY 1900s, GEORGIA HAD THE LARGEST JEWISH POPULATION IN THE SOUTH AND MANY OF THESE GEORGIAN JEWS WERE ABLE TO TRACE THEIR LINEAGES AS FAR BACK AS THEIR GENTILE NEIGHBORS. MOST TOWNS HAD THEIR JEWISH MERCHANTS, AND FEW URBAN SOUTHERNERS GAVE THE JEWISH PRESENCE MUCH THOUGHT.

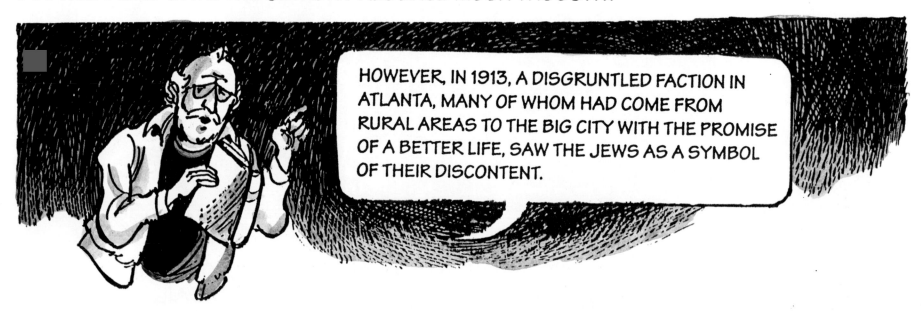

HOWEVER, IN 1913, A DISGRUNTLED FACTION IN ATLANTA, MANY OF WHOM HAD COME FROM RURAL AREAS TO THE BIG CITY WITH THE PROMISE OF A BETTER LIFE, SAW THE JEWS AS A SYMBOL OF THEIR DISCONTENT.

ON CONFEDERATE MEMORIAL DAY, IN THE ATLANTA NATIONAL PENCIL COMPANY, THE BODY OF A THIRTEEN-YEAR-OLD EMPLOYEE, MARY PHAGAN, WAS FOUND BEATEN, STRANGLED, AND MUTILATED. JIM CONLEY, THE JANITOR OF THE FACTORY WITH A RECORD OF ASSAULT AND BURGLARY, WAS SEEN BY A FOREMAN WASHING BLOOD OFF HIS SHIRT ON THE NIGHT OF THE MURDER. HOWEVER, CONLEY CLAIMED THAT LEO FRANK, THE JEWISH MANAGER OF THE FACTORY, HAD CONFESSED THE CRIME TO HIM AND HAD FORCED HIM TO WRITE A NOTE CONFESSING TO THE MURDER, WHICH WAS FOUND BESIDE THE BODY. NUMEROUS WITNESSES CORROBORATED FRANK'S STATEMENT THAT HE WAS AT HOME WITH HIS FAMILY AT THE TIME OF THE MURDER.

THE STORY WAS BIZARRE, BUT SOLICITOR GENERAL HUGH M. DORSEY HAD RECENTLY LOST A CASE AGAINST TWO MURDERERS AND HIS REPUTATION WAS SULLIED. THE CONVICTION OF AN AFFLUENT NEW YORK JEW FOR THE MURDER OF A SOUTHERN WHITE GIRL WOULD ADVANCE HIS CAREER.

UPON THE RECOMMENDATION OF HUGH DORSEY, LEO FRANK WAS CHARGED WITH THE CRIME AND HELD WITHOUT BAIL. THE ENSUING TRIAL WAS BOTH A SHAM AND A SHAME.

HELD IN AN ATMOSPHERE OF ANTI-SEMITIC VIOLENCE, THE TRIAL, BOTH INSIDE AND OUTSIDE THE COURTROOM, WAS A TRAVESTY OF JUSTICE. THE JURY WAS THREATENED WITH DEATH IF IT DIDN'T BRING IN A VERDICT OF GUILTY AND THE JUDGE WAS THREATENED WITH DEATH IF HE DIDN'T PASS A SENTENCE OF DEATH BY HANGING.

THE JURY DELIBERATED FOR FOUR HOURS. LEO FRANK WAS CONVICTED ON THE TESTIMONY OF JIM CONLEY AND SENTENCED TO DEATH BY HANGING. A CAMPAIGN TO OVERTHROW THE CONVICTION WAS LAUNCHED BY JEWISH LEADERS. THEY HIRED THE CELEBRATED PRIVATE DETECTIVE, WILLIAM BURNS, WHO UNCOVERED EVIDENCE IN FRANK'S FAVOR THAT WAS SUPPRESSED BY PROSECUTOR DORSEY. FRANK'S LAWYERS APPEALED TO GOVERNOR JOHN SLATON, WHO COMMUTED THE SENTENCE TO IMPRISONMENT FOR LIFE.

GOVERNOR SLATON ISSUED THIS STATEMENT . . .

TWO THOUSAND YEARS AGO, ANOTHER GOVERNOR WASHED HIS HANDS OF A CASE AND TURNED OVER A JEW TO A MOB. IF TODAY ANOTHER JEW WERE LYING IN HIS GRAVE BECAUSE I HAD FAILED TO DO MY DUTY, I WOULD ALL THROUGH LIFE FIND HIS BLOOD ON MY HANDS AND WOULD CONSIDER MYSELF AN ASSASSIN THROUGH COWARDICE.

ON AUGUST 16, 1915, A VIGILANTE MOB BROKE INTO A PRISON NEAR MACON, GEORGIA, DRAGGED FRANK FROM HIS CELL, AND LYNCHED HIM.

IN 1982, ALONZO MANN CAME FORWARD TO SAY THAT HE SAW JIM CONLEY DRAG THE VICTIM'S CORPSE TO THE BASEMENT OF THE PENCIL FACTORY. MANN HAD KEPT SILENT BECAUSE CONLEY THREATENED TO KILL HIM.

IN 1986, THE STATE OF GEORGIA POSTHUMOUSLY PARDONED LEO FRANK.

IN 1914, THE JEWISH SOCIALIST FEDERATION, ALONG WITH OTHER ETHNIC-IMMIGRANT ANTIWAR GROUPS, DEMONSTRATED AGAINST "CAPITALIST BLOOD-LETTING" IN EUROPE . . .

THE WAR IS BEING FOUGHT ON THE BODIES OF THE WORKING PEOPLE OF EUROPE

AMERICA STAY OUT!

DON'T HELP THE BLOODY TZAR!

IT WASN'T UNTIL 1917, WITH THE SUCCESSFUL OVERTHROW OF THE TZARIST REGIME BY THE BOLSHEVIKS, THAT JEWISH RELUCTANCE TO JOIN THE ALLIES CHANGED. WITH THE BRUTAL REPRESSION OF RUSSIAN JEWS A THING OF THE PAST, AMERICAN JEWS WERE NOW EAGER TO SUPPORT AMERICA'S ENTRY INTO THE WAR.

JACOB SCHIFF, AT A MEETING OF THE AMERICAN LEAGUE OF JEWISH PATRIOTS, DECLARED . . .

I LOVE THE GERMAN PEOPLE. BUT I DO NOT LOVE THE GERMAN GOVERNMENT AS IT EXISTS TODAY. WE MUST WIN THE WAR AND FOREVER BANISH THE IMPERIALISTIC PRINCIPLE OF THE KAISER AND HIS COHORTS.

AMERICA ENTERED THE WAR ON APRIL 6, 1917— LESS THAN A MONTH AFTER THE RUSSIAN REVOLUTION.

AMERICAN LEAGUE OF JEWISH PATRIOTS

LEON TROTSKY (1897-1940), A RUSSIAN JEW, WAS BORN LEV DAVIDOVICH BRONSTEIN. AT THE START OF THE BOLSHEVIK REVOLUTION, HE WAS LIVING IN EXILE WITH HIS FAMILY AT 1522 VYSE AVENUE IN THE BRONX, NEW YORK, AND WORKING AS AN ACTOR AT THE SILENT MOVIE STUDIO ON DECATUR AVENUE. LENIN SUMMONED HIM OUT OF EXILE TO RETURN TO RUSSIA, WHERE HE BECAME SECOND IN COMMAND AND ORGANIZED THE RED ARMY. RUSSIAN JEWS REJOICED THAT ONE OF THEIR OWN WAS IN HIGH OFFICE AND BELIEVED THAT LIFE FOR THEM WOULD IMPROVE. BUT WHEN LENIN DIED, JOSEPH STALIN SEIZED OFFICE AND TROTSKY WAS ONCE AGAIN FORCED INTO EXILE.

AT THE TIME THAT TROTSKY WAS FIGHTING HIS REVOLUTION THE UNITED STATES WAS GEARING UP FOR WAR . . .

PRESIDENT WILSON MADE BERNARD BARUCH CHAIRMAN OF THE WAR INDUSTRIES BOARD. AT THE TIME, BARUCH, SON OF SIMON BARUCH, THE RENOWNED CONFEDERATE ARMY SURGEON, WAS A FINANCIAL ADVISER TO THE PRESIDENT. GIVEN THE AUTHORITY TO MOBILIZE AMERICAN INDUSTRIAL POWER, BARUCH RECRUITED EXPERIENCED BUSINESS EXECUTIVES—KNOWN AS DOLLAR-A-YEAR-MEN (A TITLE BARUCH INVENTED)—TO COORDINATE PRODUCTION TO MEET WAR NEEDS WHILE KEEPING A LID ON LABOR COSTS AND CORPORATE PROFITS.

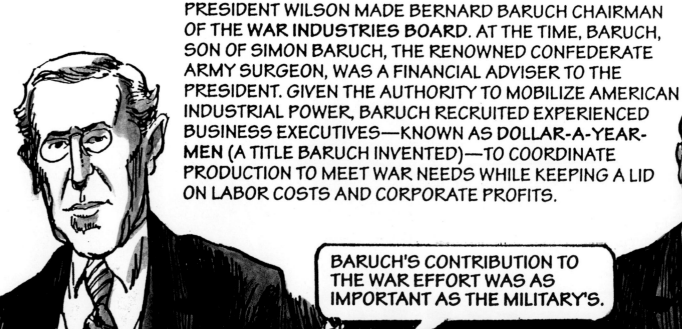

BARUCH'S CONTRIBUTION TO THE WAR EFFORT WAS AS IMPORTANT AS THE MILITARY'S.

WOODROW WILSON (1856-1924)
28TH PRESIDENT OF THE UNITED STATES

BERNARD BARUCH (1870-1965)
AMERICAN JEW AND FINANCIER

WHILE IT WASN'T AS RAPID FOR NATIVE-BORN AMERICANS, THE ACCEPTANCE OF THE WAR FOR THE THOUSANDS OF IMMIGRANT JEWS WAS COMPARABLE TO THAT OF OTHER IMMIGRANT GROUPS. THE 77TH ("MELTING POT") DIVISION WAS COMPRISED OF RECRUITS SPEAKING FORTY-TWO DIFFERENT LANGUAGES. ITS CELEBRATED "LOST BATTALION" WAS CUT TO SHREDS IN THE GERMANS' LAST OFFENSIVE OF THE WAR.

FORTY PERCENT OF THE LOST BATTALION WERE LOWER EAST SIDE JEWS.

THE NEW YORK TRIBUNE PUBLISHED A MOVING TRIBUTE TO THE JEWS OF THE LOST BATTALION UNDER THE TITLE "TO HESTER STREET."

IN CONTRAST TO THE TZAR'S ARMY, WHICH WOULD HAVE REPAID HIS SERVICE WITH PERSECUTION, THE "SWEATSHOP POET," MORRIS ROSENFELD, WROTE OF HIS AMERICAN EXPERIENCE ...

THE ARMY OF THE UNITED STATES IS WILLING TO ACCEPT ME AS AN EQUAL CITIZEN IN ITS JUST WAR.

IN 1918, 3.3 PERCENT OF THE COUNTRY'S POPULATION WAS JEWISH AND 5.7 PERCENT OF THEM SERVED IN THE ARMED FORCES. OF THE 250,000 JEWISH SOLDIERS AND SAILORS, 51,000 WERE ENLISTEES. THIRTY-FOUR HUNDRED WERE KILLED IN ACTION; 14,000 WERE WOUNDED; AND OF THE 1,130 WHO WERE AWARDED MEDALS, FOUR RECEIVED THE NATION'S HIGHEST DECORATION FOR VALOR, THE MEDAL OF HONOR.

BUT STALIN TOOK OVER AFTER LENIN DIED, AND TROTSKY WAS EXILED. ZAYDEH'S DREAM OF A WORKERS' PARADISE NEVER CAME TO BE—AND FROM THEN ON HE BECAME A GRUMPY OLD MAN WANDERING THE FIELDS ALONE AND TALKING TO HIMSELF.

THERE WERE LOTS OF LETTERS FROM PAPA. HE WROTE THAT AMERICA WASN'T REALLY A GOLDEN LAND—BUT COMPARED TO RUSSIA IT WAS PARADISE!

PAPA SENT US MONEY TO COME TO AMERICA ALONG WITH A TINTED PHOTO OF HIMSELF WEARING A RED, WHITE, AND BLUE-STRIPED BOW TIE AND A STRAW HAT. THE BAND ON HIS HAT WAS ALSO RED, WHITE, AND BLUE. HE HAD SHAVED OFF HIS BEARD AND HE LOOKED LIKE A REAL AMERICAN.

AND I AM PROUD TO BE A VETERAN AFTER SERVING WITH THE NEW YORK 77TH IN FRANCE.

HE NO LONGER LOOKS LIKE ONE OF US.

WOW, HE WAS A REAL AMERICAN SOLDIER.

WE LEFT IN A HURRY, TAKING ONLY WHAT WE WERE ABLE TO CARRY. ON OUR WAY FROM MINSK TO BREMEN, WHENEVER WE CAME TO A BORDER CROSSING, MAMA WOULD UNPIN THE KNIPPLE FROM HER BOSOM, TAKE OUT SOME MONEY AND GIVE IT TO THE GUARD.

MAMA AND ZAYDEH TOOK TURNS CARRYING SARAH AS WE CREPT STEALTHILY THROUGH TOWNS THAT LOOKED DESERTED. ZAYDEH WOLFE SAID THERE WERE EYES ON US —IT WAS SPOOKY. LATER WE PASSED THROUGH VILLAGES DESTROYED BY THE WAR. I TRIED TO IMAGINE FAMILIES LIKE OURS WHO LIVED THERE.

AT LAST WE'RE IN AMERICA
the GOLDENEH MEDINEH

IT HAS BEEN DAYS SINCE WE LEFT BREMEN. OUR SHIP IS ANCHORED IN NEW YORK HARBOR, BELCHING BLACK SMOKE, SPEWING WET CINDERS DOWN ON US, MAKING US LOOK LIKE COAL MINERS. I WAS SEASICK ALL THE WAY AS WERE ALL THE OTHER PASSENGERS EXCEPT ZAYDEH WOLFE.

I CAN STAND UP NOW WITHOUT FEELING NAUSEATED—I FEEL HUNGRY ENOUGH TO EAT!

WE WERE PUSHED AND SHOVED INTO THE BIG, SCARY-LOOKING BUILDING. ZAYDEH SAID IT SMELLED LIKE A PIGSTY. I WONDERED HOW HE KNEW WHAT A PIGSTY SMELLED LIKE.

ZAYDEH RESENTED BEING TAGGED LIKE A SACK OF POTATOES AND HERDED LIKE CATTLE THROUGH A NETWORK OF MAZES. "GOLDENE MEDINA," HE KEPT SAYING SARCASTICALLY, OVER AND OVER AGAIN, "GOLDENE MEDINA."

AFTER ELLIS ISLAND WE WERE ON A BOAT TO NEW YORK CITY. WE PASSED UNDER THE BROOKLYN BRIDGE. ZAYDEH SAID HE LIKED THE BROOKLYN BRIDGE BECAUSE IT "SERVED A PURPOSE UNLIKE THAT IDLE IDOL WITH A TORCH."

THAT MUST BE THE BIGGEST BRIDGE IN THE WORLD!

WE'VE BEEN LIVING HERE IN THE BRONX FOR FIVE YEARS...

POP AMERICANIZED OUR NAME. IN SCHOOL AND EVERYWHERE ELSE I'M SAMMY MOSCOW...

ACCORDING TO MY PUBLIC SCHOOL TEACHER, MRS. MURPHY, WE ARE ASSIMILATED!

ZAYDEH SAYS OUR LAST NAME IS NOT IMPORTANT. HE IS ZEV BEN ITZHAAK, PAPA IS YACOV BEN ZEV, AND I AM SHMUL BEN YACOV.

THERE WERE MANY, MOSTLY OLDER, FOLKS WHO COULD NOT ADJUST TO THIS NEW LAND. SOME RETURNED TO EUROPE. ZAYDEH WOLFE REMAINED, WALKING THE STREETS OF THE BRONX TALKING TO HIMSELF JUST AS HE HAD DONE IN THE FIELDS OF RUSSIA. ZEV BEN ITZHAAK DIED DISILLUSIONED IN 1924, THE YEAR OF THE NEW IMMIGRATION ACT, WHICH BARRED THE ENTRY OF EASTERN EUROPEANS (MOSTLY JEWS).

The PROTOCOLS of the ELDERS of ZION

IN 1864, MAURICE JOLY, A FRENCH JOURNALIST, PUBLISHED A POLITICAL SATIRE. THE PLOT WAS A SPOOF ABOUT A CONSPIRACY OF WORLD DOMINATION BY NAPOLEON III OF FRANCE. IN 1868, A GERMAN NOVELIST PLAGIARIZED THE WORK AND CHANGED THE PROTAGONIST FROM NAPOLEON III TO A GROUP OF JEWISH ELDERS IN PRAGUE.

IN 1905, THE TZARIST SECRET POLICE, SEEKING TO BLAME REVOLUTIONARY UNREST ON THE JEWS, EMPLOYED SERGEI NILUS TO PUBLISH YET ANOTHER VERSION ENTITLED, "THE GREAT AND THE SMALL." IN THIS NILUS VERSION, "THE WISE MEN OF ZION" FORMULATE A CONSPIRACY OF TWENTY-FOUR "PROTOCOLS" WITH WHICH TO DOMINATE THE WORLD. THE LUDICROUS SCHEME INVOLVED A COALITION OF INTERNATIONAL BANKERS AND MARXISTS SOCIALISTS.

IN 1917, AFTER THE BOLSHEVIK REVOLUTION, A GROUP OF TZARIST OFFICERS EMBELLISHED NILUS'S WORK AND PUBLISHED IT UNDER THE TITLE, "THE PROTOCOLS OF THE ELDERS OF ZION."

AN ABSURD AND DECEITFUL TRACT, "THE PROTOCOLS OF THE ELDERS OF ZION" WAS NOW WELL ON ITS WAY TO ARMING THE ANTI-SEMITIC CRACKPOTS OF THE WORLD.

1920 ENTER HENRY FORD...

A SMALL MICHIGAN NEWSPAPER, THE DEARBORN INDEPENDENT, PUBLISHED A SERIES OF ARTICLES BASED ON "THE PROTOCOLS OF THE ELDERS OF ZION," DECLARING THE EXISTENCE OF A PLOT BY INTERNATIONAL JEWISH BANKERS TO SUBVERT THE AMERICAN JUDICIAL SYSTEM.

THE PUBLISHER OF THE DEARBORN INDEPENDENT WAS NOT A RUN-OF-THE-MILL CRACKPOT BIGOT. HE WAS HENRY FORD, THE OWNER OF ONE OF THE WORLD'S MOST POWERFUL INDUSTRIAL EMPIRES.

FORD'S FAILURE TO FLOAT A BOND ISSUE THROUGH JEWISH BANKERS MIGHT HAVE INFLUENCED HIS ABIDING HATRED OF JEWS.

FORD'S ASSAULT CONTINUED WITH THE PUBLICATION OF A BOOK COMPILED OF DEARBORN INDEPENDENT ARTICLES TITLED THE INTERNATIONAL JEW. THE BOOK WAS WELL RECEIVED IN RURAL AMERICA.

CLEANSE AMERICA OF BLOOD-SUCKING JEW BANKERS!

SEND THE BOLSHEVIK JEWS BACK TO WHERE THEY CAME FROM!

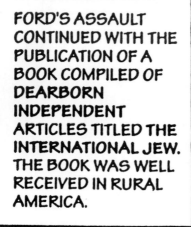

WHEN THE TIME CAME TO RETALIATE, FOUR PROMINENT AMERICAN JEWS, AARON SAPIRO, HERMAN BERSTEIN, MORRIS GEST, AND LOUIS MARSHALL, BROUGHT SUIT AGAINST HENRY FORD. THE HEARST NEWSPAPER CHAIN BRANDED FORD AN "IGNORAMUS" AS DID A MAJORITY OF MAJOR MAGAZINES.

ONE HUNDRED NINETEEN EMINENT AMERICANS HEADED BY PRESIDENT WOODROW WILSON AND FORMER PRESIDENT WILLIAM HOWARD TAFT ISSUED A MANIFESTO CONDEMNING HENRY FORD.

WHEN HE WAS SET TO RELEASE HIS NEW MODEL A, JEWS AND GENTILE FIRMS WITH JEWISH TRADE BOYCOTTED FORD PRODUCTS.

FORD'S SON, EDSEL, PLEADED WITH HIM TO END HIS ANTI-SEMITIC CAMPAIGN AND MAKE AMENDS.

DAD, WE'RE LOSING BUSINESS!

AFTER DEVIOUS AND FUTILE MEANS OF STALLING, FORD FINALLY SETTLED OUT OF COURT AND ISSUED A STATEMENT ASKING FORGIVENESS FROM JEWS FOR THE HARM HE "UNINTENTIONALLY" COMMITTED.

HOWEVER...

IN 1938, FORD ACCEPTED THE GRAND CROSS OF THE GERMAN EAGLE FROM ADOLF HITLER AND TWO YEARS LATER HE ISSUED A STATEMENT THAT "INTERNATIONAL JEWISH BANKERS" CAUSED THE OUTBREAK OF WORLD WAR II—AN OPINION SHARED BY HIS FRIEND AND EMPLOYEE, CHARLES LINDBERGH.

TZEDAKAH – PHILANTHROPY
ONE OF THE BASIC TENETS OF JEWISH DOCTRINE
JEWS ARE TAUGHT TO GIVE A PORTION OF THEIR INCOME TO CHARITY.

JUDAH TOURO
(1775-1854)
MERCHANT

FROM JUDAH TOURO (1775-1854) TO JULIUS ROSENWALD (1862-1932), SUCCESSFUL JEWS TURNED TO PHILANTHROPY TO EXPRESS THEIR GRATITUDE TO AMERICA. TOURO MADE GENEROUS CONTRIBUTIONS TO BOTH JEWISH AND GENTILE CHARITIES. IN THE CENTURIES THAT FOLLOWED, JEWS LIKE JACOB SCHIFF, SIMON GUGGENHEIM, OTTO KAHN, AND ALBERT LASKER GAVE THANKS TO AMERICA THROUGH THEIR GENEROUS PHILANTHROPY.

ALBERT LASKER
(1880-1952)

OTTO KAHN
(1867-1934)

SIMON GUGGENHEIM
(1867-1941)

JULIUS ROSENWALD
(1862-1932)

HOWEVER, NO JEWISH MILLIONAIRE COULD MATCH THE GENEROSITY AND COMPASSION OF JULIUS ROSENWALD, THE FOUNDER OF SEARS ROEBUCK. AFTER READING BOOKER T. WASHINGTON'S UP FROM SLAVERY, ROSENWALD DECIDED TO CONTRIBUTE A LARGE PORTION OF HIS ASSETS TO BLACK EDUCATION. TOGETHER, ROSENWALD, PRIVATE CITIZENS, AND THE COUNTY GOVERNMENTS IN FIFTEEN SOUTHERN STATES BUILT 5,347 BLACK SCHOOLS AND COLLEGES.

HE GAVE ME THE SHIRT OFF HIS BACK!

SHLOMO LIPSKY
(1865-1920)
TAILOR

EVEN THOSE OF LESSER MEANS PARTAKE IN TZEDAKAH.

A MUTUAL ADMIRATION

SHOLEM ALEICHEM (1859-1916) BORN SHOLEM RABINOWITZ IN THE UKRAINE

MARK TWAIN (1835-1910) BORN SAMUEL CLEMENS IN FLORIDA, MISSOURI

TEVYE

BOTH SATIRISTS ADOPTED PEN NAMES. SHOLEM ALEICHEM MEANS "PEACE BE WITH YOU," AND MARK TWAIN IS A RIVER TERM MEANING "SAFE WATER, OF A DEPTH OF TWO FATHOMS."

HUCKLEBERRY FINN

IN 1906, SHOLEM ALEICHEM EMIGRATED TO NEW YORK, WHERE HE APPEARED WITH MARK TWAIN AT THE EDUCATIONAL ALLIANCE. SHOLEM ALEICHEM ACHIEVED HIS PINNACLE OF FAME POSTHUMOUSLY WITH THE BROADWAY PRODUCTION OF **FIDDLER ON THE ROOF.** THE PLAY RAN FOR EIGHT YEARS, A RECORD FOR ITS TIME. IT DID REMARKABLY WELL IN LANGUAGES ALL OVER THE WORLD, INCLUDING FINNISH AND JAPANESE. THE ESTEEMED ACTOR, ZERO MOSTEL, IMMORTALIZED THE ROLE OF TEVYE, THE MILKMAN.

I AM CALLED THE JEWISH MARK TWAIN.

AND THEY CALL ME THE AMERICAN SHOLEM ALEICHEM.

THE 1928 PRESIDENTIAL ELECTION
A CHICKEN IN EVERY POT— A CAR IN EVERY BACKYARD!

THE TOP HAT VS. THE DERBY

THE GREAT PROSPERITY OF THE COUNTRY UNDER THE REPUBLICAN ADMINISTRATION OF PRESIDENT COOLIDGE HELPED HOOVER TO WIN HANDILY OVER SMITH.

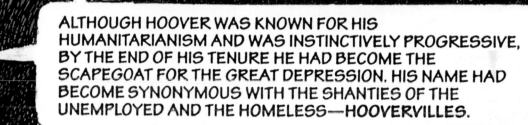

HERBERT HOOVER

AL SMITH, THE HAPPY WARRIOR

AT HOOVER'S INAUGURATION IN JANUARY OF 1929, THE NATION WAS STILL AT THE PEAK OF PROSPERITY. BUT BY OCTOBER THE MARKET HAD CRASHED, PLUNGING THE COUNTRY INTO DEEP DESPAIR.

ALTHOUGH HOOVER WAS KNOWN FOR HIS HUMANITARIANISM AND WAS INSTINCTIVELY PROGRESSIVE, BY THE END OF HIS TENURE HE HAD BECOME THE SCAPEGOAT FOR THE GREAT DEPRESSION. HIS NAME HAD BECOME SYNONYMOUS WITH THE SHANTIES OF THE UNEMPLOYED AND THE HOMELESS—HOOVERVILLES.

WHO YOU VOTIN' FOR IN THE NEXT ELECTION?

ANYBODY, AS LONG AS IT'S NOT HOOVER!

WELCOME TO HOOVERVILLE

I WAS BORN IN 1922, IN THE BRONX, NEW YORK. WARREN G. HARDING WAS PRESIDENT AND TIMES WERE PROSPEROUS. WHEN I WAS SEVEN, THE STOCK MARKET CRASHED AND A YEAR LATER THE GREAT DEPRESSION WAS UPON US.

BUT AS WITH ALL ADVERSITY, THERE WERE GLIMMERS OF OPPORTUNITY. ONE OF THE FIRST OF SUCH RECOLLECTIONS WAS THE APPEARANCE OF THE STREET SINGERS—UNEMPLOYED PROFESSIONAL MUSICIANS WHO CAME AROUND TO SING AND PLAY THEIR INSTRUMENTS IN THE BACKYARDS OF THE TENEMENTS, WHERE WE WOULD TOSS THEM HARD-EARNED PENNIES FROM OUR WINDOWS.

THE POPULAR MUSIC BUSINESS, LIKE THE GARMENT INDUSTRY, WAS ATTRACTIVE TO JEWS. POPULAR MUSIC PUBLISHING AND THE MOVIES, WHICH IN THEIR BEGINNINGS HAD A FAINT TAINT OF SCANDAL, GAINED RESPECTABILITY BECAUSE OF JEWISH ENTERPRISE. TIN PAN ALLEY, WHICH GOT ITS NAME FROM THE CACOPHONY OF TINKLING PIANOS ALONG NEW YORK'S 28TH STREET, WAS CONSPICUOUSLY JEWISH.

THE STREET SINGER WHO MADE IT IN THE BIGTIME...

ARTHUR TRACY, ONE OF THE FIRST SUPERSTARS OF RADIO, WAS A RUSSIAN-BORN JEWISH TROUBADOUR WHO BEGAN BY SINGING IN A SYNAGOGUE CHOIR. HE MADE HIS WAY TO THE YIDDISH THEATER AND THEN ONTO CBS RADIO, WHERE HE WAS BILLED AS THE STREET SINGER. TRACY BECAME A SINGING SENSATION AND HIS RECORDS SOLD IN THE MILLIONS.

TIN PAN ALLEY and THE MOVIES

SERVED AS DIVERSIONS FROM THE HARD TIMES. THE CONTRIBUTIONS OF TALENTS LIKE GEORGE GERSHWIN, ROGERS AND HAMMERSTEIN, MOSS HART, HAROLD ARLEN, DOROTHY FIELDS, FANNY BRICE, EDDIE CANTOR, AL JOLSON, THE MARX BROTHERS, SOPHIE TUCKER, AND SCORES OF OTHERS—IMMIGRANTS AND CHILDREN OF IMMIGRANTS—HELPED US THROUGH THE GRINDING GLOOM OF THE GREAT DEPRESSION.

TWO of HOLLYWOOD'S GREAT MOGULS...

ANYONE WHO GOES TO SEE A PSYCHIATRIST OUGHT TO HAVE HIS HEAD EXAMINED.

SAMUEL GOLDWYN

SAMUEL GOLDWYN WAS BORN SHMUL GOLDFISH IN POLAND IN 1882. HE IMMIGRATED TO NEW YORK AT THE AGE OF THIRTEEN AND WORKED IN A GLOVE FACTORY. WHEN HE WAS THIRTY, HE OWNED THE BUSINESS. GOLDFISH STARTED IN THE MOVIE INDUSTRY AS AN ASSOCIATE OF HIS BROTHER-IN-LAW, JESSE LASKY. HE LATER JOINED EDGAR A. SELWYN. USING HALF OF HIS NAME AND THE LAST PART OF SELWYN'S, THEY FORMED THE GOLDWYN PICTURES CORPORATION. GOLDWYN IS REMEMBERED FOR HIS GREAT CONTRIBUTION TO THE MOVIE INDUSTRY AND HIS MALAPROPISMS.

LOUIS B. MAYER WAS BORN IN RUSSIA IN 1885. IN 1907, HE BOUGHT A BURLESQUE THEATER IN MASSACHUSETTS AND BEGAN SHOWING FILMS. MAYER MOVED TO HOLLYWOOD IN 1918 AND FORMED THE LOUIS B. MAYER PICTURE CORPORATION. IN 1924, HE TEAMED UP WITH GOLDWYN AND CREATED METRO-GOLDWYN-MAYER. MAYER'S UNDERSTANDING OF PUBLIC TASTE MADE MGM HUGELY SUCCESSFUL.

GOLDWYN AND MAYER LAUNCHED MANY A HOLLYWOOD STAR'S CAREER

LOUIS B. MAYER

DUTCH SCHULTZ

"GREASY THUMB" GUZIK

"KID TWIST" RELES

CRIME...
A BYPRODUCT OF POVERTY

EVERY ETHNIC IMMIGRANT SOCIETY HAD ITS SHARE OF GANGSTERS. THE JEWISH COMMUNITY HAD AN ARRAY OF THUGS WITH NAMES LIKE "KID TWIST" RELES, DUTCH SCHULTZ, "GREASY THUMB" GUZIK, AND MANY MORE.

SLUM LIFE, WITH ITS GRINDING POVERTY AND THE DISINTEGRATION OF FAMILY AUTHORITY, PRODUCED A SPATE OF RENOWNED GANGSTERS, WHICH INCLUDED BUGSY SIEGEL AND LEPKE BUCHALTER OF THE INFAMOUS MURDER INC. MOST STARTED AS PETTY CRIMINALS AND WORKED THEIR WAY UP IN THE MOB.

AS WITH OTHER ETHNIC IMMIGRANT GROUPS, SOME JEWS SAW THEIR WAY OUT OF THE GHETTO THROUGH BOXING. BENNY LEONARD, ONE OF THE FIRST JEWISH CHAMPIONS, INSPIRED THOUSANDS OF JEWISH KIDS TO BECOME BOXERS. MAX BAER, BARNEY ROSS, SLAPSY MAXIE ROSENBLOOM, AND AL SINGER MADE IT TO THE TOP.

JEWS WERE SO REVERED IN THE SPORT THAT OTHERS WHO WERE NOT JEWS WORE A STAR OF DAVID ON THEIR TRUNKS.

A MEASURE OF COMIC RELIEF FROM THE GREAT DEPRESSION CAME FROM THE NEWSPAPER COMIC STRIP . . .

COMIC STRIPS SOLD NEWSPAPERS. JOSEPH PULITZER SAW THE VALUE OF THE CARTOONIST, AS DID WILLIAM RANDOLPH HEARST . . .

THEY BECAME COVETOUS OF EACH OTHER'S CARTOONISTS AND THEIR COMIC STRIPS. THE COMPETITION WAS RUTHLESS.

WILLIAM RANDOLPH HEARST

JOSEPH PULITZER

SOMETIMES, I MYSELF FEEL LIKE A CARTOON CHARACTER.

JEWS FIGURED PROMINENTLY AS PUBLISHERS AND CARTOONISTS IN THIS UNIQUELY AMERICAN MEDIUM.

•JOSEPH PULITZER
•FREDERIC OPPER
•RUBE GOLDBERG
•MILT GROSS
•HARRY HERSHFIELD
•MAX FLEISHER
•JERRY SIEGEL
•JOE SCHUSTER
•AL CAPP
•OTTO SOGLOW
AND ON AND ON AND ON . . .

FDR's NEW DEAL

ALTERED THE SOCIAL STRUCTURE OF THE NATION. LABOR BECAME MORE POWERFUL ECONOMICALLY AND POLITICALLY. THE COUNTRY WAS STILL IN THE GRIP OF THE DEPRESSION, BUT ROOSEVELT'S POPULARITY WAS AT ITS PEAK. HE WENT ON TO WIN AN UNPRECEDENTED FOUR PRESIDENTIAL VICTORIES.

AT THE TIME OF FDR'S DEATH IN 1945, MOST JEWS WOULD HAVE BEEN IN FAVOR OF ADDING HIS BUST TO MT. RUSHMORE.

THE PROSPECT THAT TIME WOULD REVEAL A ROOSEVELT UNWORTHY OF REVERENTIAL RESPECT WOULD HAVE BEEN UNTHINKABLE TO THE JEWS WHO SO PASSIONATELY SUPPORTED HIM.

1939 A TRAGEDY THAT COULD HAVE BEEN AVERTED...

THE LADY in the HARBOR WEPT

IN MAY 1939, THE OCEAN LINER ST. LOUIS LEFT GERMANY WITH 930 JEWISH REFUGEES SEEKING TEMPORARY ASYLUM IN CUBA WHILE WAITING FOR AMERICAN VISAS. CUBA REFUSED PERMISSION TO LAND AND THE SHIP SLOWLY CRUISED THE AMERICAN COASTLINE. WHEN ALL EFFORTS FAILED THE REFUGEES MADE THEIR LAST ATTEMPT—A DIRECT APPEAL TO THE OVAL OFFICE. ROOSEVELT LEFT THEIR TELEGRAM UNOPENED.

AS THE SHIP STEAMED BACK ACROSS THE ATLANTIC, GREAT BRITAIN, BELGIUM, FRANCE, AND THE NETHERLANDS AGREED TO PROVIDE TEMPORARY REFUGE TO ITS PASSENGERS. ULTIMATELY, MOST OF THESE JEWS SUFFERED THE FATE OF THE SIX MILLION.

NO JEWS ALLOWED

WHILE THE ST. LOUIS AFFAIR WAS DRAGGING ON, ANOTHER DRAMA INVOLVING ROOSEVELT AND THE JEWS WAS BEING PLAYED OUT: A BILL WAS INTRODUCED PERMITTING THE ADMISSION OF TWENTY THOUSAND JEWISH REFUGEE CHILDREN FROM GERMANY . . .

ELEANOR ROOSEVELT PLEADED WITH HER HUSBAND TO INTERCEDE ON BEHALF OF THE CHILDREN, BUT FDR TURNED A DEAF EAR TO HER. HE RELIED ON THE VIEWS OF HIS COUSIN, LAURA DELANO, WIFE OF HIS IMMIGRATION COMMISSIONER . . .

SHE WAS QUOTED AS SAYING "TWENTY THOUSAND CHARMING CHILDREN WOULD ALL TOO SOON TURN INTO TWENTY THOUSAND UGLY ADULTS."

BOYCOTT
UNITY
GERMAN MADE GOODS
ANTI FASCIST LEAGUE, WINNIPEG

ZIONIST LEADER RABBI STEPHEN S. WISE HAD A "BOSS-STEVE" FRIENDSHIP WITH FDR . . .

ROOSEVELT PRIVATELY ASSURED RABBI WISE THAT HE WOULD ACT TO EASE THE PLIGHT OF EUROPEAN JEWS. BUT HE WAS UNWILLING TO RISK CHALLENGING THE XENOPHOBIC ATTITUDE OF MANY INFLUENTIAL AMERICANS. SIX MILLION JEWS PERISHED. THE BELIEF IS THAT MANY COULD HAVE BEEN SAVED HAD ROOSEVELT ACTED.

1940 BELGIUM, HOLLAND, and FRANCE FALL BEFORE the NAZI BLITZKRIEG—NO WAY OUT for JEWS

AFTER THE FALL OF FRANCE, JAPAN JOINED HITLER AND MUSSOLINI TO FORM THE AXIS.

DESPITE PROTESTS FROM THE AMERICA FIRSTERS AND THEIR ILK, ROOSEVELT GOT THE **LEND-LEASE** AND THE **DRAFT BILLS** THROUGH CONGRESS. AMERICA WAS ABLE TO SUPPLY ARMAMENTS TO BRITAIN. JEWISH MEN IN LARGE NUMBERS WERE SERVING IN THE UNITED STATES ARMED FORCES.

THROUGH LEND-LEASE, BRITAIN WAS ABLE TO OBTAIN SOME OF THE MOTHBALLED U.S. NAVAL FLEET.

WINSTON CHURCHILL'S COMMENT ON THE BATTLE OF BRITAIN . . .

IT WAS THEIR FINEST HOUR.

WHEREAS ROOSEVELT GAVE AMERICANS "NOTHING TO FEAR BUT FEAR ITSELF," PRIME MINISTER WINSTON CHURCHILL OFFERED THE BRITISH "BLOOD, SWEAT, AND TEARS." THE DEFEAT OF HITLER'S LUFTWAFFE ALLOWED AMERICAN BOMBERS TO SOFTEN UP GERMAN-OCCUPIED EUROPE FOR THE "D-DAY" INVASION.

CASUALTIES WERE HIGH. OF THE NINETEEN JEWISH GENERALS IN THE AMERICAN ARMY, MAJOR GENERAL MAURICE ROSE, THE SON OF A RABBI WHO COMMANDED THE THIRD ARMORED DIVISION IN THE NORMANDY BREAKTHROUGH, WAS KILLED IN ACTION.

ALTHOUGH CHURCHILL WAS KNOWN TO BE "FOND OF JEWS," HE FAILED, AS DID ROOSEVELT, TO BOMB THE GAS CHAMBERS AND THE RAILWAY LINES LEADING TO AUSCHWITZ. HOWEVER, CHURCHILL STRONGLY AND OPENLY SUPPORTED ZIONISM AND THE ESTABLISHMENT OF ISRAEL.

ELEVEN PERCENT OF THE JEWISH POPULATION SERVED IN THE UNITED STATES ARMED FORCES DURING WORLD WAR II, SLIGHTLY HIGHER THAN THE NATIONAL AVERAGE. TWENTY-NINE PERCENT OF THOSE SERVED IN THE ARMY AIR CORPS. ONE IN FIVE WERE PILOTS. THERE WERE THIRTY-FIVE THOUSAND JEWISH CASUALTIES, INCLUDING TEN THOUSAND DEATHS. THIRTY-SIX THOUSAND WON DECORATIONS.

BUT THE AREA IN WHICH JEWISH CONTRIBUTION WAS UNIQUE AND DECISIVE WAS IN THE BUILDING OF THE ATOMIC BOMB. THE MANHATTAN PROJECT WAS HEAVILY STAFFED WITH JEWISH PHYSICISTS—MOSTLY REFUGEES WHO HAD ESCAPED HITLER'S FINAL SOLUTION. PHYSICISTS LEO SZILARD AND EUGENE WIGNER CONVINCED THE GREAT EINSTEIN TO WRITE TO PRESIDENT ROOSEVELT APPRISING HIM OF THE PROBABILITY OF BUILDING A WORKABLE ATOMIC BOMB. ECONOMIST ALEXANDER SACHS HAND-DELIVERED THE LETTER TO FDR.

NIELS BOHR

EDWARD TELLER

1945

EINSTEIN WAS HORRIFIED AT THE NOTION OF DROPPING AN ATOMIC BOMB ON JAPANESE CIVILIANS, ESPECIALLY WHEN HE THOUGHT THE DEFEAT OF JAPAN WAS IMMINENT. EINSTEIN DISPATCHED SZILARD WITH A LETTER TO THE NEW PRESIDENT, HARRY S. TRUMAN ...

ROBERT OPPENHEIMER

ALBERT EINSTEIN

TRUMAN REFERRED SZILARD TO HIS SECRETARY OF STATE, HARRY BYRNES. BYRNES WAS UNRECEPTIVE. THE BOMB WAS DROPPED.

WHEN THE ASHES OF WAR CLEARED . . .
THE HOLOCAUST
SIX MILLION WERE MURDERED FOR NO OTHER REASON THAN BEING JEWISH.
42309
OF THE SIX MILLION, ONE AND ONE-HALF MILLION WERE CHILDREN.
ANNE FRANK

THE RIGHTEOUS GENTILES

FROM 1933 TO 1943, THOUSANDS OF JEWS WERE SAVED FROM EXTERMINATION BY "RIGHTEOUS GENTILES" WHO RISKED THEIR LIVES OUT OF COMPASSION. ONE OF THE MOST NOTABLE WAS A SWEDISH BANKER, RAOUL WALLENBERG, WHO SAVED THOUSANDS OF HUNGARIAN JEWS. WALLENBERG WAS LAST SEEN IN 1945, ACCOMPANIED BY A RUSSIAN OFFICER. RUSSIAN OFFICIALS CLAIM THAT HE DIED OF NATURAL CAUSES IN 1947, IN A SOVIET FORCED LABOR CAMP.

BALFOUR DECLARATION

MANY JEWS ESCAPING NAZI PERSECUTION TOOK REFUGE IN PALESTINE UNTIL ARAB OPPOSITION TO ZIONISM ESCALATED. TO ASSUAGE THE ARABS, THE BRITISH PUT A STRICT QUOTA ON JEWISH IMMIGRATION. MANY BOATLOADS OF JEWS WERE TURNED BACK TO NAZI-OCCUPIED EUROPE.

EXODUS

THE GERMANS DESTROYED OUR HOMES AND FAMILIES. DON'T LET THE BRITISH DESTROY OUR HOPES

ROOSEVELT DIED DURING WORLD WAR II IN AN UNPRECEDENTED FOURTH TERM IN OFFICE. UNLIKE FDR, VICE PRESIDENT TRUMAN, WHO ASSUMED THE PRESIDENCY IN 1945, LOST LITTLE TIME IN APPEALING TO BRITAIN TO ALLOW ONE HUNDRED THOUSAND JEWISH REFUGEES TO ENTER PALESTINE.

EVERYONE ELSE WHO'S BEEN DRAGGED FROM HIS COUNTRY HAS SOMEPLACE TO GO BACK TO, BUT THE JEWS HAVE NO PLACE TO GO.

WHEREAS ROOSEVELT BOASTED OF MANY FRIENDS WHO WERE JEWISH, TRUMAN CLAIMED BUT ONE, HIS FORMER PARTNER IN A FAILED KANSAS CITY HABERDASHERY BUSINESS, EDDIE JACOBSON. AT A CRITICAL TIME IN JEWISH HISTORY, THE UNASSUMING JACOBSON WOULD FIGURE PROMINENTLY.

YES   DA

UNITED STATES   SOVIET UNION

JACOBSON URGED HIS OLD FRIEND TO MEET WITH ZIONISM'S ELDER STATESMAN, CHAIM WEIZMANN, BEFORE THE UNITED NATIONS VOTE ON THE PARTITION OF PALESTINE. WEIZMANN CONVINCED TRUMAN THAT THE TIME WAS AT HAND FOR A JEWISH HOMELAND.

IT WAS ONE OF THE RARE MOMENTS IN THE HISTORY OF THE UNITED NATIONS—THE UNITED STATES AND THE SOVIET UNION VOTED IN AGREEMENT.

TRUMAN WAS COURTING THE JEWISH VOTE.

I DOUBT IT.

STALIN WAS HOPING FOR A SOCIALIST ALLY IN THE MIDDLE EAST.

PERHAPS.

ISRAEL'S WAR of INDEPENDENCE

AS SOON AS THE ISRAELI FLAG WAS RAISED THE ARAB NATIONS SURROUNDING THE FLEDGLING STATE BEGAN AN ALL-OUT ATTACK.

JEWS WHO HAD SURVIVED THE HOLOCAUST, SABRAS, AND JEWISH-AMERICANS FRESH FROM WORLD WAR II RALLIED AND DEFEATED THE COMBINED FORCES OF JORDAN, EGYPT, AND SYRIA.

LIEUTENANT-COLONEL DAVID DANIEL MARCUS (1902-1948)

MARCUS, A JEWISH-AMERICAN GRADUATE OF WEST POINT, PARTICIPATED IN THE AIRBORNE INVASION OF NORMANDY ON D-DAY.

IN 1948, HE BECAME MILITARY ADVISOR TO DAVID BEN GURION UNDER THE NOM DE GUERRE, MICKEY STONE. MARCUS WAS APPOINTED COMMANDER OF THE JERUSALEM FRONT AND KEPT THE SUPPLY LINES OPEN TO THE ANCIENT CITY.

MARCUS WAS ACCIDENTALLY KILLED BY AN ISRAELI SENTRY.

1956 The EGYPTIAN THREAT to the INFANT DEMOCRACY

EGYPT'S DICTATOR, GAMAL ABDEL-NASSER, WITH $200 MILLION WORTH OF SOVIET-RUSSIAN ARMS, WAS DETERMINED TO DESTROY ISRAEL. HE SEIZED THE SUEZ CANAL AND BLOCKADED THE GULF OF AQABA, FURTHER TIGHTENING THE NOOSE AROUND THE FLEDGLING STATE'S NECK. WHEN BEN GURION ASKED PRESIDENT EISENHOWER FOR ARMS TO DEFEND HIS YOUNG DEMOCRACY, EISENHOWER'S REPLY WAS . . .

HOW CAN 1.7 MILLION JEWS DEFEND THEMSELVES AGAINST 40 MILLION ARABS?

IMPOSSIBLE!

BRITAIN AND FRANCE, TO PROTECT THEIR OWN INTERESTS IN THE AREA, SOLD ARMS TO ISRAEL AND JOINED IN A STRIKE AGAINST EGYPT. ISRAEL WON THE SINAI AND THE GAZA STRIP. EISENHOWER WAS FURIOUS AND URGED ISRAEL TO RETURN THE CONQUERED TERRITORY. THE UNITED NATIONS PROMISED TO PROTECT ISRAEL'S SECURITY.

ISRAEL CANNOT LIVE ON PROMISES. WE MUST BE READY TO DEFEND OURSELVES.

AND AS EXPECTED

JEWS THE WORLD OVER, WHO HAD BEEN BANNED BY JORDAN FROM WORSHIPING AT THE WESTERN WALL, WERE NOW FREE TO DO SO—AND AMERICANS WERE CHOOSING THE WESTERN WALL AS THE SITE OF THEIR BAR-MITZVAHS.

1973 The YOM KIPPUR WAR

ON YOM KIPPUR, 1973—THE HOLIEST DAY OF THE YEAR—EGYPT'S PRESIDENT, ANWAR AL-SADAT, LAUNCHED HIS ARMED FORCES AGAINST ISRAEL WITH DEADLY SURPRISE AS SYRIAN FORCES STRUCK FROM THE EAST. THE PRIME MINISTER OF ISRAEL, GOLDA MEIR, WAS SHAKEN BY THE DANGEROUS LOSSES INFLICTED IN THE FIRST FEW DAYS. ISRAEL NEEDED REPLACEMENT WEAPONS FAST AND THE ONLY COUNTRY CAPABLE OF SUPPLYING THEM WAS THE UNITED STATES.

MADE IN USSR

GOLDA MEIR

BUT RICHARD M. NIXON WAS PRESIDENT . . .

The CIVIL RIGHTS MOVEMENT

JEWS HAD ACHIEVED THEIR POLITICAL AND ECONOMIC BREAKTHROUGH AND WERE READY TO JOIN AFRO-AMERICANS IN ACHIEVING THEIRS.

1965 The VOTING RIGHTS ACT

MICHAEL SCHWERNER AND ANDREW GOODMAN, TWO YOUNG NEW YORKERS, SERVED AS VOTER REGISTRATION VOLUNTEERS IN MISSISSIPPI ALONG WITH JAMES CHANEY, A LOCAL, YOUNG, BLACK MAN. THE THREE MEN WERE BRUTALLY MURDERED BY KLANSMEN WHO DUMPED THEIR BODIES IN A HASTILY DUG GRAVE. IT WAS THE NATIONAL REVULSION OVER THE DISCOVERY OF THEIR BODIES THAT HASTENED THE PASSAGE OF THE VOTING RIGHTS ACT OF 1965.

ALTHOUGH SOUTHERN JEWS KEPT A LOW PROFILE ON CIVIL RIGHTS, KLAN GROUPS CONDUCTED A CAMPAIGN OF VIOLENCE AGAINST THEM. TEMPLES AND JEWISH COMMUNITY CENTERS WERE BOMBED AND RABBIS RECEIVED DEATH THREATS.

IT WAS THE OPEN PARTICIPATION OF NORTHERN JEWS IN THE CIVIL RIGHTS MOVEMENT THAT PRECIPITATED THESE ANTI-SEMITIC ACTS.

JEWS WERE IN THE FOREFRONT IN THE ESTABLISHMENT OF THE NATIONAL ASSOCIATION FOR THE ADVANCEMENT OF COLORED PEOPLE. JOEL SPINGARN, A RETIRED COLUMBIA PROFESSOR, BECAME CHAIRMAN AND RECRUITED JACOB SCHIFF AND RABBI STEPHEN WISE FOR ITS BOARD.

NAACP

HARLEM WAS A HEAVILY POPULATED JEWISH COMMUNITY BEFORE AFRICAN-AMERICANS MOVED IN. BUILDINGS AND SHOPS WERE LARGELY OWNED AND OPERATED BY JEWS. WHEN THEY LEFT THE ENCLAVE, SOME JEWS HELD ON TO THEIR OWNERSHIP AND OPERATION OF BUSINESSES AND REAL ESTATE. THE IMAGE OF THE JEWISH OVERLORD FED BLACK RESENTMENT.

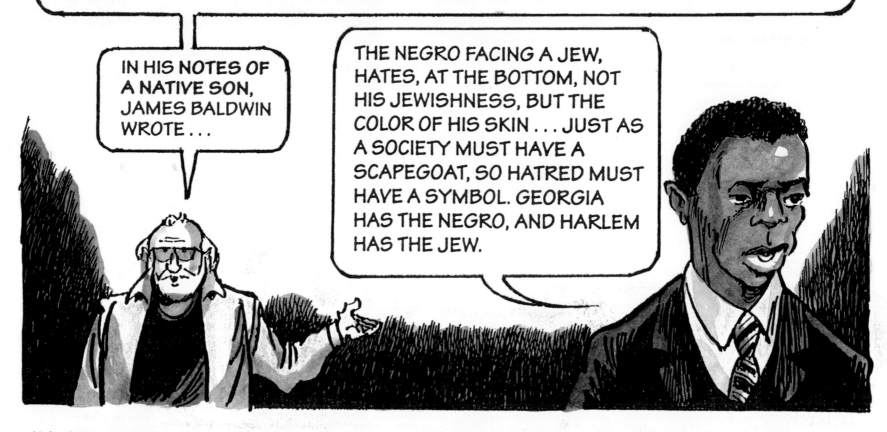

IN HIS NOTES OF A NATIVE SON, JAMES BALDWIN WROTE . . .

THE NEGRO FACING A JEW, HATES, AT THE BOTTOM, NOT HIS JEWISHNESS, BUT THE COLOR OF HIS SKIN . . . JUST AS A SOCIETY MUST HAVE A SCAPEGOAT, SO HATRED MUST HAVE A SYMBOL. GEORGIA HAS THE NEGRO, AND HARLEM HAS THE JEW.

IN THE BEGINNING, THE JEW WAS THE NEGRO'S LINK TO WHITE SOCIETY. AS THINGS PROGRESSED, THE BLACKS WANTED THEIR OWN VOICE. MILITANTS BEGAN TO REGARD JEWISH INVOLVEMENT AS PATRONIZING.

LOUIS FARRAKHAN OF THE NATION OF ISLAM ONCE SHOCKED THE JEWISH COMMUNITY WITH HIS ANTI-SEMITIC PEJORATIVES. BUT FARRAKHAN HAS SINCE RECANTED. THERE IS AN ONGOING CONCERTED EFFORT BY JEWS AND BLACKS TO RETURN TO THEIR COOPERATIVE RELATIONSHIP OF THE PAST.

The FEMINIST MOVEMENT

LONG BEFORE BETTY FRIEDAN (THE FEMININE MYSTIQUE), BELLA ABZUG (CONGRESSWOMAN), AND GLORIA STEINEM (MS. MAGAZINE) CAME UPON THE SCENE, THERE WAS ERNESTINE POTOVSKY ROSE (1810-1982).

BORN IN POLAND, THE DAUGHTER OF AN ORTHODOX RABBI, ERNESTINE TRAVELED TO ENGLAND, WHERE SHE BECAME A MEMBER OF THE OWENITES, AN ENGLISH REFORM MOVEMENT. IN 1836, SHE MARRIED WILLIAM ROSE AND IMMIGRATED TO NEW YORK. SHE LECTURED ON ABOLITION, FREE SCHOOLING, AND WOMEN'S RIGHTS. ALONG WITH ELIZABETH CADY STANTON AND SUSAN B. ANTHONY, ERNESTINE POTOVSKY ROSE HELPED ORGANIZE THE FIRST NATIONAL WOMEN'S RIGHTS CONVENTION IN 1848.

THE FEMINIST MOVEMENT HAS RESHAPED THE AMERICAN FAMILY. WOMEN HAVE GONE FROM THEIR TRADITIONAL POSITION AS THE KEEPERS OF THE HEARTH TO THEIR RIGHTFUL POSITION ALONGSIDE MEN IN THE WORKPLACE. IT HAS ALSO ENABLED MEN TO FIND THEIR INNATE NURTURING ABILITIES. BUT THE RATE OF SINGLE-PARENT FAMILIES HAS ESCALATED AND THERE ARE THOSE WHO BEMOAN THIS STATE OF FLUX . . .

WILL WOMEN AND MEN FIND A WAY TO DEAL WITH THE CHANGING FAMILY STRUCTURE IN THE TWENTY-FIRST CENTURY?

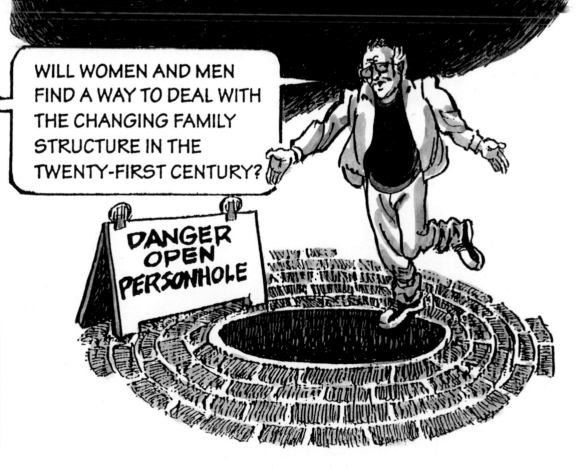

DANGER OPEN PERSONHOLE

VIETNAM war and The NEW LEFT

IN THE TROUBLED SIXTIES, THE **NEW LEFT** INVADED THE COUNTRY'S CAMPUSES. ITS IMPETUS WAS THE "MORALISTIC CONDEMNATION" OF THE VIETNAM WAR AND THE HYPOCRISY OF THE SOCIO-POLITICAL SYSTEM. SIT-INS, CONFRONTATIONS, AND DISRUPTIONS WERE NOTICEABLY PRESENT IN THE VANGUARD.

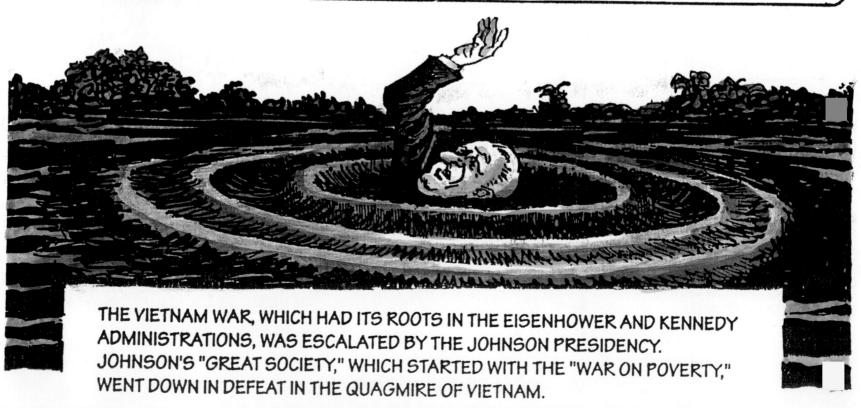

THE VIETNAM WAR, WHICH HAD ITS ROOTS IN THE EISENHOWER AND KENNEDY ADMINISTRATIONS, WAS ESCALATED BY THE JOHNSON PRESIDENCY. JOHNSON'S "GREAT SOCIETY," WHICH STARTED WITH THE "WAR ON POVERTY," WENT DOWN IN DEFEAT IN THE QUAGMIRE OF VIETNAM.

SAVING SOVIET JEWRY

1967

ROMANIAN PRESIDENT NICOLAE CEAUSESCU WAS PAID EIGHT THOUSAND DOLLARS PER HEAD BY A CONSORTIUM OF JEWISH-AMERICAN AGENCIES TO ALLOW ROMANIAN JEWS TO EMIGRATE TO ISRAEL.

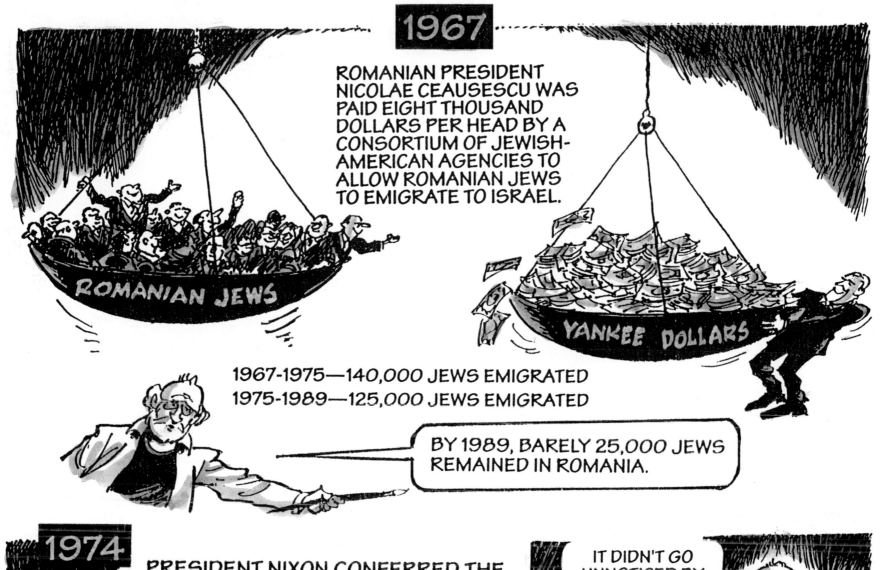

1967-1975—140,000 JEWS EMIGRATED
1975-1989—125,000 JEWS EMIGRATED

BY 1989, BARELY 25,000 JEWS REMAINED IN ROMANIA.

1974

PRESIDENT NIXON CONFERRED THE MOST-FAVORED NATION STATUS ON ROMANIA.

IT DIDN'T GO UNNOTICED BY THE RUSSIAN BEAR

THE MORE AMBITIOUS TARGET WAS THE THIRD LARGEST JEWISH POPULATION IN THE WORLD: TWO MILLION SOVIET JEWS.

COURAGEOUS AMERICAN JEWS MADE TRIPS TO RUSSIA TO CONTACT REFUSENIKS. AMERICAN CHILDREN CELEBRATING THEIR BAR AND BAT MITZVAHS WERE PAIRED WITH THEIR RUSSIAN COUNTERPARTS.

RECOGNIZING HOW EAGER THE SOVIETS WERE FOR MOST-FAVORED NATION STATUS, AMERICAN JEWS LOBBIED CONGRESS TO APPLY PRESSURE . . .

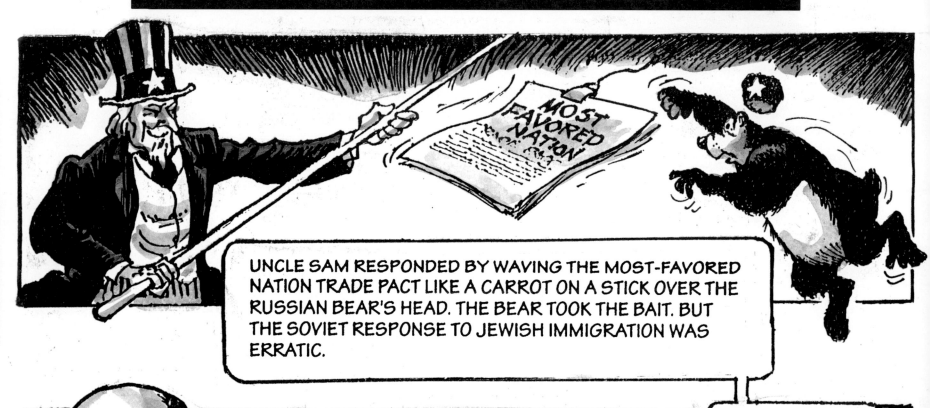

UNCLE SAM RESPONDED BY WAVING THE MOST-FAVORED NATION TRADE PACT LIKE A CARROT ON A STICK OVER THE RUSSIAN BEAR'S HEAD. THE BEAR TOOK THE BAIT. BUT THE SOVIET RESPONSE TO JEWISH IMMIGRATION WAS ERRATIC.

NATAN (ANATOLY) SHARANSKY (B. 1948) UKRAINIAN JEW

SHARANKSY WAS THE FOREMOST DISSIDENT AND SPOKESMAN FOR THE SOVIET JEWRY MOVEMENT. IN 1973, HE APPLIED FOR AN EXIT VISA TO ISRAEL BUT WAS REFUSED ON "SECURITY" GROUNDS. HE THEN BECAME INVOLVED IN REFUSENIK ACTIVITIES. SHARANSKY WAS SENTENCED TO PRISON FOR TREASON AND CONFINED TO THE NOTORIOUS SIBERIAN GULAG.

BETWEEN 1977 AND 1980, 106,774 SOVIET JEWS EMIGRATED. FROM 1980 TO 1989, 37,866.

SHARANSKY BECAME A SYMBOL FOR HUMAN RIGHTS AND SOVIET JEWRY. IN 1986, HE WAS RELEASED AS PART OF AN EAST-WEST PRISONER EXCHANGE. WHEN HE ARRIVED IN ISRAEL HE WAS GREETED BY PRIME MINISTER SHIMON PERES. FROM 1996 TO 1999, SHARANSKY SERVED ISRAEL AS ITS MINISTER OF INDUSTRY AND TRADE.

MEANWHILE . . .

RUSSIAN JEWS WERE RECEIVING LETTERS FROM ISRAEL

AND AMERICA WAS BECOMING THE FAVORED CHOICE

GRISHA SAYS IT'S NOT MILK AND HONEY, IT'S NO UTOPIA. IT'S NO AMERICA!

UNDER THE TERMS OF THE MCCARRAN-WALTER ACT, REFUGEES FROM COMMUNISM WERE PERMITTED TO ENTER THE U.S. ON A PRIORITY BASIS . . .

WELCOME, WELCOME!

OF THE 106,774 SOVIET-JEWISH EMIGRANTS BETWEEN 1977 AND 1980, 66,414 CHOSE THE UNITED STATES.

IN 1989, THE WALL THAT SEPARATED COMMUNIST EAST GERMANY AND DEMOCRATIC WEST GERMANY WAS TORN DOWN. THE SOVIET UNION COLLAPSED AND IT BECAME EASIER FOR JEWS TO EMIGRATE.

1974 The **WATERGATE SCANDAL** FORCED NIXON TO RESIGN. VICE PRESIDENT GERALD FORD TRIPPED INTO OFFICE AND RETAINED NIXON'S SECRETARY OF STATE, HENRY KISSINGER. IT WAS THE CLOSEST A JEW—EVEN AN ASSIMILATED ONE—EVER GOT TO RUNNING THE INTERNATIONAL AFFAIRS OF THE UNITED STATES.

GERALD FORD

HENRY KISSINGER

1978 AFTER COMPLETING HIS REMAINING THREE YEARS IN OFFICE, FORD LOST TO JIMMY CARTER, WHO TOOK OFFICE WITH A BROAD SMILE AND HANDICAPPED HIMSELF BY PROCLAIMING TO THE NATION . . .

I WILL NEVER LIE TO YOU.

A POLITICIAN WHO DOESN'T LIE—DOES THAT QUALIFY AS AN OXYMORON?

NEVERTHELESS, IN SEPTEMBER OF 1978, JIMMY CARTER WOULD BROKER AN AGREEMENT THAT WOULD HAVE A PROFOUND EFFECT ON HIS JEWISH CONSTITUENCY.

The CAMP DAVID ACCORD—

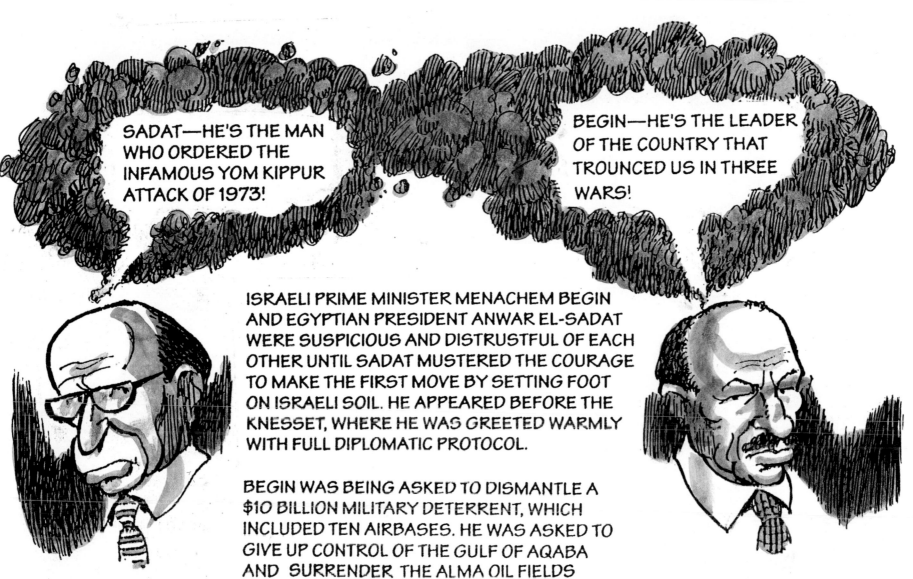

SADAT—HE'S THE MAN WHO ORDERED THE INFAMOUS YOM KIPPUR ATTACK OF 1973!

BEGIN—HE'S THE LEADER OF THE COUNTRY THAT TROUNCED US IN THREE WARS!

ISRAELI PRIME MINISTER MENACHEM BEGIN AND EGYPTIAN PRESIDENT ANWAR EL-SADAT WERE SUSPICIOUS AND DISTRUSTFUL OF EACH OTHER UNTIL SADAT MUSTERED THE COURAGE TO MAKE THE FIRST MOVE BY SETTING FOOT ON ISRAELI SOIL. HE APPEARED BEFORE THE KNESSET, WHERE HE WAS GREETED WARMLY WITH FULL DIPLOMATIC PROTOCOL.

BEGIN WAS BEING ASKED TO DISMANTLE A $10 BILLION MILITARY DETERRENT, WHICH INCLUDED TEN AIRBASES. HE WAS ASKED TO GIVE UP CONTROL OF THE GULF OF AQABA AND SURRENDER THE ALMA OIL FIELDS IN THE SINAI, WHICH ISRAEL HAD DEVELOPED AT A COST OF $5 BILLION.

MENACHEM BEGIN

ANWAR EL-SADAT

IT'S A LAND-FOR-PEACE DEAL, MENACHEM.

WOULD HE GIVE TEXAS AND CALIFORNIA BACK TO MEXICO IF I ASKED HIM?

IT WAS A TALL ORDER, BUT IT MEANT PEACE WITH ISRAEL'S MOST POWERFUL ARAB NEIGHBOR.

A FRAGILE ACCORD WAS REACHED AT CAMP DAVID

IN THE MONTHS FOLLOWING, WITH SADAT AND BEGIN BACK IN CAIRO AND JERUSALEM, THE ACCORD BEGAN TO FALL APART.

TO SAVE THE AGREEMENT, PRESIDENT CARTER EMBARKED UPON A GRUELING WEEK OF SHUTTLING BETWEEN JERUSALEM AND CAIRO. THE PRESIDENT, AT ONE POINT, BECAME SO DESPERATE THAT HE EVEN CONSIDERED GETTING THE SOVIET UNION INVOLVED IN THE PEACEMAKING.

BUT MORE PRUDENT HEADS PREVAILED AND A FINAL PEACE TREATY WAS HAMMERED OUT.

1979 The CAMP DAVID PEACE TREATY IS SIGNED...

IT WAS CARTER'S FINEST MOMENT. THE NOBEL PEACE PRIZE WENT TO MENACHEM AND ANWAR—JIMMY WAS JUSTIFIABLY MIFFED.

1985 RONALD REAGAN DEFEATS JIMMY CARTER

ISRAEL IS A STABILIZING FORCE AND A MILITARY COUNTER-BALANCE TO SOVIET INFLUENCE.

THE CARTER ADMINISTRATION'S DECISION TO ABSTAIN INSTEAD OF VETOING THE U.N.'S CONDEMNATION OF ISRAEL'S PROCLAMATION OF JERUSALEM AS ITS CAPITAL ANGERED REAGAN—AND THROUGHOUT HIS TENURE, ISRAEL HAD A FRIEND IN THE WHITE HOUSE . . .

EXCEPT FOR ➡

1985 BITBURG— GERMAN CHANCELLOR HELMUT KOHL INVITED PRESIDENT REAGAN TO LAY A WREATH IN A GERMAN MILITARY CEMETERY . . .

WHEN IT WAS LEARNED THAT THE INFAMOUS WAFFEN SS TROOPS WERE BURIED THERE, HOLOCAUST SURVIVOR ELIE WIESEL MADE AN ELOQUENT PLEA FOR REAGAN TO REFUSE THE INVITATION.

I UNDERSTAND YOUR PAIN, MR. WIESEL, BUT I MADE A COMMITMENT TO OUR NATO ALLY.

WHAT ABOUT OUR COMMITMENT TO COMMON DECENCY?

REAGAN WENT TO BITBURG, BUT IT REMAINED THE ONLY BLEMISH ON AN OTHERWISE AMICABLE RELATIONSHIP WITH HIS JEWISH CONSTITUENCY.

RONALD REAGAN WAS SUCCEEDED BY GEORGE W. BUSH, WHOSE ROOTS WERE STEEPED IN OIL.

I PROMISE TO PROTECT OUR INTERESTS IN THE MIDDLE EAST.

HENCE, BUSH WAS NOT AS FAVORABLY DISPOSED TO ISRAEL AS REAGAN.

BUSH'S SHINING MOMENT WAS "DESERT STORM," WHICH PUSHED THE INVADING IRAQI FORCES OUT OF KUWAIT AND SAVED SAUDI ARABIA. THE ARAB STATES WERE BEHOLDEN TO BUSH . . .

BUT HE FAILED TO SEIZE THIS PROPITIOUS MOMENT TO GET THESE APPRECIATIVE ARAB STATES TO MAKE PEACE WITH ISRAEL, WHICH STAYED OUT OF THE WAR DESPITE IRAQI SCUD MISSILE ATTACKS ON ITS CITIES.

GENERAL COLIN POWELL, CHAIRMAN OF THE JOINT CHIEFS OF STAFF

ISRAEL HAD SURVIVED THE PAST FORTY YEARS BY TAKING NO GUFF FROM ITS ENEMIES . . . AND IT WAS CLEAR TO OUR SIDE THAT WE HAD TO KEEP ISRAEL OUT OF THIS WAR. THE FORBEARANCE OF THE ISRAELIS, IN THE FACE OF INTENSE PROVOCATIONS, GOING COMPLETELY AGAINST THEIR GRAIN, IN MY JUDGMENT HELPED KEEP OUR COALITION INTACT.

1993 The SIGNING OF THE OSLO ACCORD...

PRESIDENT BILL CLINTON, BUSH'S SUCCESSOR, WATCHED AS RABIN AND ARAFAT SHOOK HANDS ON A DECLARATION OF PRINCIPLES FOR PALESTINIAN AUTONOMY IN THE WEST BANK AND GAZA. PRESENT ON THE WHITE HOUSE SOUTH LAWN WERE HENRY KISSINGER, JESSE JACKSON, LUBAVITCHER JEWS, AND OTHER DIGNITARIES.

WHEN CONFRONTED BY ARAB DETRACTORS, ARAFAT COUNTERED WITH . . .

HOLY JERUSALEM WILL BE THE CAPITAL OF THE PALESTINIAN STATE!

WHEN CRITICIZED FOR HIS RECOGNITION OF THE PLO, RABIN REPLIED . . .

YOU DON'T MAKE PEACE WITH FRIENDS, YOU MAKE IT WITH ENEMIES.

1995

YITZHAK RABIN IS ASSASSINATED BY A YOUNG ISRAELI EXTREMIST.

A NATION MOURNS

YITZHAK RABIN 1922-1995

HEAR, O ISRAEL, LEST WE BECOME WHAT WE DESPISE!

RABIN'S SUCCESSOR, BENJAMIN NETANYAHU, AND BILL CLINTON WERE AT LOGGERHEADS FROM THE START. AND ALTHOUGH THE WYE RIVER ACCORD WAS PUT ON THE TABLE AND A PEACE TREATY WITH JORDAN WAS SIGNED DURING THEIR TENURES, THE ACCOMMODATION WITH THE PALESTINIANS REMAINED IN LIMBO.

1999 EHUD BARAK TOOK OFFICE AS PRIME MINISTER OF ISRAEL. TENSIONS BETWEEN THE UNITED STATES AND ISRAEL EASED.

PRESIDENT CLINTON WENT TO OSLO TO PRESIDE OVER YET ANOTHER HANDSHAKE, THIS TIME BY BARAK AND ARAFAT, IN AN EFFORT TO RESTART THE PEACE PROCESS.

HOW MANY MORE HANDSHAKES WILL IT TAKE?

AS 1999 WAS DRAWING TO A CLOSE, PRESIDENT CLINTON ENVISIONED A CAMP DAVID-STYLE SUMMIT IN THE YEAR 2000 FOR THE FINAL SIGNING OF THE OSLO PEACE TREATY.

MEANWHILE

ORGANIZED HATE GROUPS WERE AT WORK STIRRING UP RACISM AND ANTI-SEMITISM IN THEIR HIGH-TECH CAULDRON—THE INTERNET.

ANYONE CAN KEY INTO BIGOTRY

BUFORD O. FURROW

> THOSE PROMOTING HATE, RACIAL VIOLENCE, AND TERRORISM HAVE BEEN ABLE TO DO SO DIRECTLY INTO THE MAINSTREAM, 24 HOURS A DAY, SEVEN DAYS A WEEK.

RABBI ABRAHAM COOPER OF THE SIMON WIESENTHAL CENTER

AUGUST 10, 1999

BUFORD O. FURROW, A WHITE SUPREMACIST, OPENED FIRE AT A JEWISH COMMUNITY CENTER, WOUNDING THREE CHILDREN, A TEENAGER, AND A SIXTY-EIGHT-YEAR-OLD RECEPTIONIST. LATER THAT DAY HE SHOT AND KILLED A LATINO POSTAL WORKER.

> THE FIRST AMENDMENT OF THE CONSTITUTION OF THE UNITED STATES MAKES IT POSSIBLE FOR BUFORD FURROW AND HIS ILK TO ACCESS AND DISSEMINATE HATE PROPAGANDA . . .

> HOWEVER, THIS VERY SAME CONSTITUTION MAKES THE UNITED STATES OF AMERICA THE FREEST AND SAFEST HAVEN FOR THE JEW IN THE DIASPORA.

JEWISH CONTRIBUTIONS TO CONTEMPORARY AMERICAN CULTURE

SO MANY JEWISH WRITERS WERE BEING SUCCESSFULLY PUBLISHED DURING THE POST-WORLD WAR II ERA THAT IT LED CRITIC GEORGE STEINER TO WRITE IN A 1975 NEW YORKER ARTICLE, "IT IS A COMMONPLACE THAT RECENT AMERICAN FICTION AND CRITICISM HAVE TO A DRASTIC EXTENT BEEN THE PRODUCT OF JEWISH TONE AND EXPLOSION OF TALENT," TO WHICH ALFRED KAZIN ADDED, "DEFINITELY, IT WAS NOW THE THING TO BE JEWISH."

CYNTHIA OZICK (B. 1928)

HER BRILLIANT SHORT STORIES BROUGHT A NEW INTELLECTUAL SOPHISTICATION TO THE EXPLORATION OF JEWISH THEMES IN AN AMERICAN SETTING.

BERNARD MALAMUD (1914-1986)

HE WAS THE FIRST POSTWAR NOVELIST OF NOTE TO UTILIZE JEWISH PERSONAE AND SUBJECTS. HE WAS AWARDED THE PULITZER PRIZE AND TWO NATIONAL BOOK AWARDS.

NORMAN MAILER (B. 1923)

HIS NOVEL, THE NAKED AND THE DEAD, WAS THE FIRST CLASSIC NOVEL OF WORLD WAR II. THEREAFTER, MAILER DEVOTED MUCH OF HIS TIME TO ESTABLISHING HIMSELF AS THE MACHO MAN OF JEWISH WRITERS.

JOSEPH HELLER (1923-1999)

HIS BLACK-HUMOR NOVEL, CATCH-22, IS CONSIDERED TO BE THE MAJOR WAR NOVEL OF THE CENTURY.

PHILLIP ROTH
PORTNOY'S COMPLAINT

CHAIM POTOK
THE CHOSEN

SOME OF THE MANY AWARD-WINNING WRITERS INCLUDE E. L. DOCTOROW, NEIL SIMON, LEON URIS, MARGE PIERCY, HERMAN WOUK, NOAH GORDON, BEN HECHT, HENRY ROTH, ERICA JONG, PHILLIP ROTH, HOWARD FAST, ALFRED KAZIN, FANNIE HURST, BRUCE JAY FRIEDMAN, EDNA FERBER, TILLIE OLSON, ALLEN GINSBERG, HERBERT GOLD, DELMORE SCHWARTZ, CALVIN TRILLIN, WOODY ALLEN, GRACE PALEY, JERZY KOSINSKI . . .

TWO NOBEL PEACE LAUREATES

HENRY A. KISSINGER (B. 1923)

BORN IN BAVARIA, KISSINGER IMMIGRATED TO AMERICA IN 1938. IN WORLD WAR II HE WON A BRONZE MEDAL FOR INTELLIGENCE WORK BEHIND ENEMY LINES. KISSINGER BECAME THE FIRST JEW TO SERVE AS SECRETARY OF STATE, A POSITION HE HELD UNDER THE NIXON AND FORD ADMINISTRATIONS.

IN 1973, KISSINGER WAS AWARDED THE NOBEL PEACE PRIZE FOR ARRANGING THE VIETNAM WAR CEASE-FIRE.

SILENCE ENCOURAGES THE TORMENTORS, NEVER THE TORMENTED.

ELIE WIESEL (B. 1928)

ELIE WIESEL WAS BORN IN ROMANIA TO ORTHODOX PARENTS. WIESEL WAS A HOLOCAUST SURVIVOR WHO BECAME A SPOKESMAN FOR SOVIET JEWS AND OTHER OPPRESSED PEOPLES OF THE WORLD. HE BECAME AN AMERICAN CITIZEN IN 1963 AFTER COVERING WORLD NEWS FOR THE FRENCH PRESS. IN 1985, HE RECEIVED THE CONGRESSIONAL GOLD MEDAL FOR HUMANITARIAN ACHIEVEMENT AND IN 1986, THE NOBEL PEACE PRIZE.

"ELIE WIESEL IS A SPIRITUAL LEADER IN AN AGE OF VIOLENCE AND HATRED AND HAS EMBRACED ALL REPRESSED RACES AND PEOPLES."

— THE NOBEL COMMITTEE —

HERE ARE THE NAMES OF BUT A FEW OF THE MANY WHO HAVE WON THE NOBEL PRIZE IN VARIOUS FIELDS OF ENDEAVOR...

DAVID BALTIMORE
GERALD EDELMAN
MELVIN CALVIN
JULIUS AXELROD
GEORGE WALD
JOSEPH ERLANGER
HERBERT S. GASSER
ARTHUR KORNBERG
ROSALYN S. YALOW
KENNETH J. ARROW
HERMAN I. MULLER
JOSHUA LEDERBERG
DANIEL NATHANS
ALBERT EINSTEIN
MILTON FRIEDMAN
BURTON RICHTER
JULIAN S. SCHWINGER
HOWARD M. TEMIN
RICHARD P. FEYNMAN
MURRAY GELL-MANN
MARSHALL NIRENBERG
ROBERT HOFSTADTER
DONALD A. GASSER
ALBERT SABIN

NOBEL LAUREATES... LITERATURE

SAUL BELLOW (B. 1915)

BORN IN CANADA TO RUSSIAN IMMIGRANT PARENTS WHO LATER MOVED ON TO THE UNITED STATES, BELLOW GREW UP IN CHICAGO. COMPARED TO HIS CONTEMPORARIES, HE SEEMED MORE ENDOWED WITH THE TRADITIONAL JEWISH BACKGROUND, BUT HE CHOSE THE SECULAR WORLD INSTEAD OF TALMUDIC SCHOLARSHIP. HOWEVER, HE REMAINED AS FLUENT IN YIDDISH AS HE WAS IN FRENCH AND ENGLISH. HIS FIRST NOVEL, DANGLING MAN, EVOKED SOME CRITICAL ACCLAIM. AFTER A STINT IN THE MERCHANT MARINE HE SETTLED IN NEW YORK. BELLOW WENT ON TO WIN TWO NATIONAL BOOK AWARDS AND IN 1976, THE NOBEL PRIZE. HIS KEEN GRASP OF YIDDISH ENABLED HIM TO TRANSLATE SOME OF I. B. SINGER'S MANUSCRIPTS INTO ENGLISH.

ALONG WITH THE CELEBRATION OF HUMAN DIGNITY, SINGER'S STORIES ARE INHABITED BY GOBLINS AND DEMONS.

YIDDISH IS THE ONLY LANGUAGE NEVER SPOKEN BY MEN IN POWER.

SINGER WAS AWARDED THE NOBEL PRIZE IN 1978.

ISAAC BASHEVIS SINGER (1904-1991)

BORN IN POLAND, SINGER IMMIGRATED TO AMERICA, WHERE HE WROTE FOR THE YIDDISH FORVERTS. MANY OF HIS BOOKS REVOLVED AROUND THE LIFE OF THE SHTETL. I. B. SINGER'S TALENT LAY IN HIS SUBTLE CHARACTERIZATION OF HUMAN KIND WITH ALL THEIR FOIBLES, VIRTUES, SUFFERING, AND PATHOS—BUT MOST OF ALL IN HIS HUMOR, IRONY, AND WIT.

PROBLEMS of CONTEMPORARY AMERICAN JUDAISM

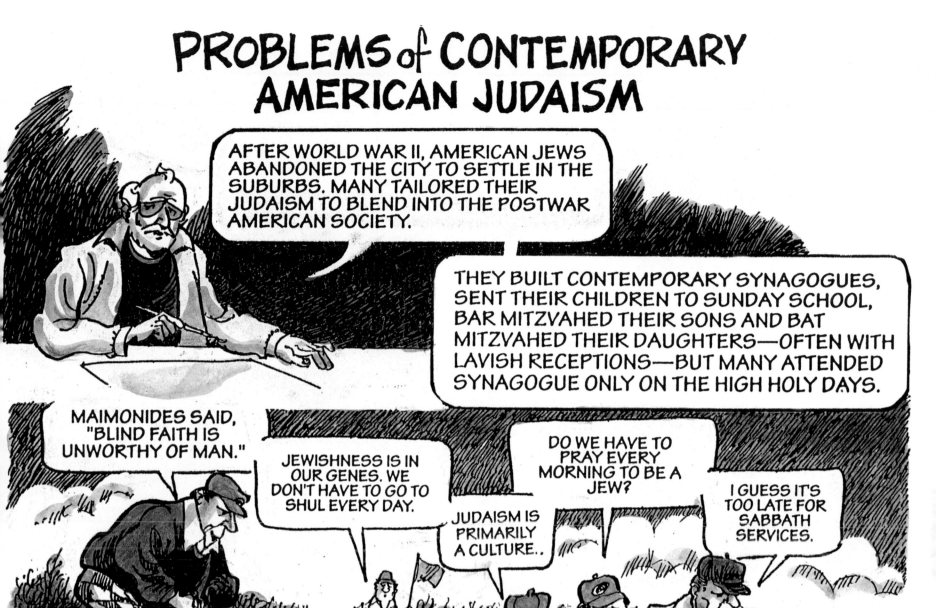

AFTER WORLD WAR II, AMERICAN JEWS ABANDONED THE CITY TO SETTLE IN THE SUBURBS. MANY TAILORED THEIR JUDAISM TO BLEND INTO THE POSTWAR AMERICAN SOCIETY.

THEY BUILT CONTEMPORARY SYNAGOGUES, SENT THEIR CHILDREN TO SUNDAY SCHOOL, BAR MITZVAHED THEIR SONS AND BAT MITZVAHED THEIR DAUGHTERS—OFTEN WITH LAVISH RECEPTIONS—BUT MANY ATTENDED SYNAGOGUE ONLY ON THE HIGH HOLY DAYS.

MAIMONIDES SAID, "BLIND FAITH IS UNWORTHY OF MAN."

JEWISHNESS IS IN OUR GENES. WE DON'T HAVE TO GO TO SHUL EVERY DAY.

JUDAISM IS PRIMARILY A CULTURE..

DO WE HAVE TO PRAY EVERY MORNING TO BE A JEW?

I GUESS IT'S TOO LATE FOR SABBATH SERVICES.

THE ORTHODOX BELIEVED THAT STRICT ADHERENCE WAS JUDAISM'S SALVATION

DRIVING TO SHUL ON THE HIGH HOLY DAYS?

THEY MUST BE ROSH HASHANAH JEWS!

MUCH HAS HAPPENED SINCE THE ORIGINAL PUBLICATION OF *JEWS IN AMERICA*. THIS ADDITION PICKS UP FROM WHERE WE LEFT OFF AND TAKES US THROUGH FIVE YEARS OF HISTORY—FIVE YEARS THAT WILL HAVE A PROFOUND EFFECT ON JEWS IN AMERICA.

JULY 2000 CAMP DAVID...

DISSATISTFIED WITH THE CONCESSIONS PUT FORTH BY THE PRIME MINISTER OF ISRAEL, EHUD BARAK, YASSIR ARAFAT STORMED OUT OF THE CAMP DAVID NEGOTIATIONS HOSTED BY PRESIDENT CLINTON. THE EFFECT WAS TANTAMOUNT TO THE SCUTTLING OF OSLO ACCORD...

YASSIR, WE ARE HERE TO NEGOTIATE.

SEPT 2000 THE DEMISE OF THE OSLO ACCORD USHERED IN THE **SECOND INTIFADA**, STARTING WITH ROCK-THROWING AT JEWS WORSHIP-PING AT WESTERN WALL...

AND ESCALATED TO THE SUICIDE-BOMBING OF JEWISH COMMUNITIES.

TO THE WESTERN WORLD...

ARAFAT REACTED TO THE SECOND INTIFADA WITH DUPLICITY.

TO THE ARAB WORLD...

I CONDEMN IT!

I CONDONE IT!

THE 2000 CAMPAIGN FOR THE 43RD PRESIDENT OF THE UNITED STATES OF AMERICA...

THE REPUBLICAN PARTY NOMINATED TEXAS GOVERNOR GEORGE W. BUSH AND RUNNING MATE, DICK CHENEY, WHO HAD BEEN SECRETARY OF DEFENSE TO BUSH'S FATHER WHEN HE SERVED AS PRESIDENT DURING GULF WAR I. CHENEY LATER BECAME CEO OF HALIBURTON, THE NO-BID SUPPLIER OF GOODS AND SERVICES IN GULF WAR II.

DEMOCRATS NOMINATED VICE PRESIDENT AL GORE, AN ACTIVE ECOLOGY PROPONENT, AND FOR HIS RUNNING MATE, THE SENATOR FROM CONNECTICUT JOSEPH LIEBERMAN, THE FIRST JEWISH AMERICAN TO BE NOMINATED FOR VICE PRESIDENT.

GORE'S HANDLERS FELT THAT HE WAS NOT GETTING THROUGH TO THE AVERAGE JOE AND THEY TRIED TO REDO HIS IMAGE.

WHICH ONE OF HIM ARE YOU GONNA VOTE FOR?

THE CONSTANT CHANGES IN GORE'S PERSONA MADE VOTERS WARY.

AUG 2002 BRENT SCOWCROFT, NATIONAL SECURITY ADVISER TO BUSH'S FATHER DURING GULF WAR I, APPEARING ON A SUNDAY NEWSCAST...

PRESIDENT BUSH KEPT PUSHING FOR A PREEMTIVE, AND IF NECESSARY, UNILATERAL STRIKE AGAINST IRAQ.

YOU ARE EITHER WITH US OR AGAINST US!

AN ATTACK ON IRAQ WOULD SERIOUSLY JEOPARDIZE, IF NOT DESTROY, THE GLOBAL COUNTER-TERRORIST CAMPAIGN WE HAVE UNDERTAKEN.

2003 DESPITE HIS THEN SECRETARY OF STATE, COLIN POWELL'S, WARNING...

IF YOU BREAK IT, YOU OWN IT.

ON MARCH 19, 2003, AMERICANS WATCHED A DAZZLING DISPLAY OF FIREWORKS ON TV CALLED...

"SHOCK and AWE."

AMERICAN BOMBS RAINED DOWN ON IRAQ...

WHERE IN 200 C.E. ISRAELITE SCHOLARS CREATED THE BABYLONIAN TALMUD.

SIGNALING THE START OF

GULF WAR II

DRESSED IN TOP-GUN REGALIA, BUSH WAS HELICOPTERED TO THE CARRIER LINCOLN, RETURNING FROM THE WAR ZONE. THERE HE ADDRESSED A CHEERING THRONG BENEATH A HUGE BANNER PROCLAIMING ...

MISSION ACCOMPLISHED ➡️

THERE WAS NO SUCH CELEBRATION IN IRAQ, WHERE OUR TROOPS WERE EXPERIENCING THE START OF ... **THE INSURGENCY.**

PRESIDENT GEORGE W. BUSH RESPONDED TO THE INSURGENCY WITH ➡️

BRING 'EM ON!

THE INSURGENTS RESPONDED TO BUSH'S RESPONSE WITH A FURIOUS ESCALATION OF SUICIDE BOMBINGS, HOSTAGE TAKING, AND BARBARIC BEHEADINGS—

FURTHER DESTABILIZING A CRITICALLY UNSTABLE MIDEAST...

THE MISSION REMAINED FAR FROM ACCOMPLISHED

THERE WERE NO WEAPONS OF MASS DESTRUCTION.

SEPT 2003 — **TORAHS for JEWISH TROOPS...**

THE JEWISH CHAPLAINS COUNCIL SENT FOUR TORAHS TO IRAQ AND KUWAIT. SENATOR HILLARY RODHAM CLINTON ARRANGED FOR THE TRANSPORTATION AND INSURANCE.

THE TORAHS ARRIVED IN TIME FOR THE ROSH HASHANA AND YOM KIPPUR CELEBRATIONS.

NOV 2004 — **"ACADEME'S MIDEAST WARS"...**

JEWISH STUDENTS AT COLUMBIA UNIVERSITY PROTEST ANTI-ISRAEL POLICIES TAUGHT IN THE MIDDLE EAST STUDIES DEPARTMENT...

IS IT POSSIBLE TO TEACH ANTI-ISRAEL COURSES WITHOUT BEING LABELED ANTI-SEMITIC?

THESE COURSES SHOULD BE TAUGHT WITH FACTUAL, UNBIASED, HISTORICAL CONTENT, DEVOID OF CURRENT PRO OR CON OPINION.

The GAZA PULLOUT

IN SOME SETTLEMENTS ISRAELI SOLDIERS WEPT WITH SETTLERS AS THEY PEACEFULLY FORCED THEM OUT.

ISRAELI SOLDIERS WEEPING? THEY DIDN'T WEEP WHEN THEY BULLDOZED OUR HOMES.

IN OTHER SETTLEMENTS SOLDIERS WERE GREETED WITH VIOLENCE...

DON'T ATTACK OUR MEN AND WOMEN IN UNIFORM. I AM RESPONSIBLE!

PRIME MINISTER ARIEL SHARON.

PALESTINIANS SHOULD NOT REJOICE AT THE SUFFERING IN GAZA.

ELIE WIESEL

WHEN THE PULLOUT WAS COMPLETED, PALESTINIANS REJOICED AND BURNED VACATED SYNAGOGUES. HAMAS PROCLAIMED A MILITARY VICTORY.

TWO AND A HALF YEARS AFTER "MISSION ACCOMPLISHED," MESOPOTAMIA, THE CRADLE OF CIVILIZATION (PRESENTLY KNOWN AS IRAQ), HAS BECOME THE PRIMARY PROVING GROUND FOR PRESENT AND FUTURE TERRORISTS …

1908-2005 **SIMON WIESENTHAL**

THE NAZI HUNTER

HIS STATED AIM WAS TO BRING NAZI WAR CRIMINALS TO JUSTICE.

WIESENTHAL LOST 89 MEMBERS OF HIS FAMILY TO THE HOLO-CAUST. HE SURVIVED THE DEATH CAMPS AND SWORE NEVER TO FORGET. HE HELPED TRACK DOWN MORE THAN 1,000 NAZI WAR CRIMINALS, INCLUDING THE INFAMOUS ADOLF EICHMANN.

SEPT 2005 *THE GROWING THREAT of ANTISEMITISM...*

IT IS HARD TO BELIEVE THAT 60 YEARS AFTER THE TRAGEDY OF THE HOLOCAUST ANTI-SEM-ITISM CONTINUES TO REAR ITS HEAD … THIS TIME WE MUST NOT—CANNOT BE SILENT.

SECRETARY-GENERAL OF THE UNITED NATIONS, KOFI ANNAN, SPEAKING AT A MEMORIAL FOR SIMON WIESENTHAL (SEPTEMBER 27, 2005).